LESSONS KIDS NEED TO LEARN

Also by David Staal

Words Kids Need to Hear

Leading Your Child to Jesus

Making Your Children's Ministry the Best Hour of Every Kid's Week (Sue Miller with David Staal)

LESSONS KIDS NEED TO LEARN

SIX TRUTHS TO SHAPE THE CHARACTER OF THE CHILD YOU LOVE

DAVID STAAL

ZONDERVAN.com/
AUTHORTRACKER
follow your favorite authors

ZONDERVAN

Lessons Kids Need to Learn
Copyright © 2012 by David Staal

This title is also available as a Zondervan ebook. Visit www.zondervan.com/ebooks.

Requests for information should be addressed to:

Zondervan, *Grand Rapids, Michigan 49530*

Library of Congress Cataloging-in-Publication Data

Staal, David.
     Lessons kids need to learn : six truths to shape the character of the child you
love / David Staal.
          p. cm.
     Includes bibliographical references (p. 149–154).
     ISBN 978-0-310-32605-2 (softcover)
     1. Parenting—Religious aspects—Christianity. 2. Child rearing—Religious
aspects—Christianity. 3. Self-esteem in children. I. Title.
BV4529.S725 2011
248.8'45—dc23   2011044324

Cover Design: Tammy Johnson
Cover Photo: Masterfile
Interior design: Matthew Van Zomeren
Editorial team: Ryan Pazdur, Bob Hudson, Leigh Clouse, Britta Eastburg

Printed in the United States of America

12 13 14 15 16 17 18 19 /DCI/ 21 20 19 18 17 16 15 14 13 12 11 10 9 8 7 6 5 4 3 2 1

To the focus-group parents and students:
From your heart, to these pages, and into readers' hearts—
your experiences, thoughts, and words
will guide others as they help kids be
who God made them to be.

CONTENTS

Pairs, Parents, and Kids

If parents want to give their children a gift, the best thing they can do is teach their children to love challenges, be intrigued by mistakes, enjoy effort, and keep on learning.
Carol S. Dweck, PhD[1]

On the day before Becky and I wed, my grandpa asked if I wanted advice about how to have a working, happy marriage. He and my grandmother had stuck together for many decades until death parted them, so I eagerly listened.

"There are two things you should do," he said. "God gave both of you opinions, so work hard to always find common ground on issues. That will help your marriage work well."

"Okay, Grandpa," I said, "what's the second thing?"

With a wink and a chuckle he said, "Always go with her opinion."

Sage advice no matter which side of the aisle you stand on. While I found his counsel profound at that moment—and for over two decades of marriage have done my best to live up to that advice—I have also learned that the roots of Grandpa's two-halves-of-the-same-equation wisdom significantly preceded his marriage.

Consider the direction given to the first couple, Adam and Eve. To paraphrase, God told them: You are free to eat anywhere in the garden, but leave the tree in the center alone. Enjoy the gift of an intimate relationship, yet bond with only one. Work hard, then take a day and relax.

From the genesis of mankind through today, we require guidance to help us become who God made each of us to be. And just as they did in the beginning, lessons imparting essential wisdom often travel in pairs. On its own, each individual lesson sounds great, but learn one without the other and you might easily travel toward an extreme, toward a life without balance.

Again, let's consider Eden. Take just one side of each of the pairs mentioned earlier and picture what would eventually happen:

- Work hard without rest—wear out and die from exhaustion.
- Relax without the hard work—fall short of your God-given potential.
- The gift of intimacy with no exclusivity—risk health, life, and love.
- An exclusive bond with no intimacy—let's not go there in this book.

Had Adam and Eve only heard instructions about the tree, they might have starved. We know that in the end, unfortunately, they took their freedom to eat too far (with the help of a slippery tempter) and ignored the boundary aspect of this lesson.

Likewise, it is critically important for today's parents to recognize that important pairs of lessons exist that, when taught in tandem, will help children achieve life-thriving balance and avoid unhealthy excesses. Looking for and teaching complementary lessons can help children grow into the young people their parents dream they will become—mature individuals who live a God-honoring life.

Lessons Kids Need to Learn is designed to provide you with insight on how to best teach your children such high-priority pairs of lessons. Each chapter contains two complementary lessons, along with the important-to-understand relationship that exists between them. Practical tips and everyday examples provide ideas that will enable you to put these lessons into practice as soon as you have read each chapter. While many books rely on counsel from credentialed experts only, this book also offers a practical, hands-on approach proven by experienced parents.

Parenting's Real Experts

The best parenting advice to come my way has typically emerged from trial and error; specifically, the successes and failures from other parents. So, as part of the research for this book, my wife, Becky, conducted focus groups made up of actual moms and dads at various locations across the country. While I observed from the back of each room, she facilitated in-depth discussions among parents with only one common, and treasured, characteristic—experience.

> The way of fools seems right to them, but the wise listen to advice. (Proverbs 12:15)

All these veteran moms and dads have children in their teens or older, so they know what they're talking about. All had plenty to share about what worked and what didn't, what they did well and what they would change, accidental successes and painful regrets. As I listened to people bravely pour out their stories, I was reminded of an observation from famed journalist and author Studs Terkel. "I've been astonished too often," he said, "by those I've visited: ordinary Americans, who, at times, are extraordinary in their insights and dreams."[2]

We encouraged openness and candor among these parents with a commitment to change every parent's and child's name in any story shared in the book. The only real names used are those of our own family members — with their permission, of course.

This promise of anonymity also encouraged participation from a second valuable group. While the focus-group parents described why and how they taught the lessons in this book, my kids, fourteen-year-old Erin and seventeen-year-old Scott, conducted focus groups with fellow teenagers. Those students willingly provided unique perspectives on how kids learned these same lessons.

Erin and Scott took a unique approach to this task, conducting virtual focus groups via Facebook. As a result, you'll often read affirming or challenging words straight from students, just as they typed them. To most authentically voice a collective youth-originated message to readers, one student wrote a challenging lesson for parents to serve as this book's Final Word.

To protect the teenagers' identities, no identifying references (gender indication, names, or ages) appear with their comments. After all, it takes a brave young person to say, "When all I hear is correction, life starts to feel like a mistake." It is imperative that we protect that kind of candor.

And one more important note, this one about gender: All lessons apply equally to boys and girls. To minimize wordiness, each story will reference either a male pronoun or its female equivalent, but throughout, the general use of one or the other implies both. As a parent of a son and daughter whose perspectives are equally valuable, I tried to balance gender references throughout the book.

Why These Lessons?

While an exhaustive list of topics to teach kids might fill an entire library, *Lessons Kids Need to Learn* focuses on six pairs of critical truths to share—along with the three foundational lessons every kid needs to learn. The fifteen lessons in total, all strongly affirmed by our focus-group parents, emerged from my three highly differentiated areas of personal experience.

In seven years as the children's ministry director for Willow Creek Community Church and the Willow Creek Association, I fielded questions every week from parents and small group leaders who worked directly with kids. In this role, I was privileged to lead a team of people who tirelessly sought to understand children, how they learn, and the biblical truths that help "train up a child in the way he should go" (Proverbs 22:6, KJV).

Now, as president of the national mentoring organization KIDS HOPE USA, I work every day in the deep gap between childhood as it ought to be and the life-draining challenges that today's children and families too often face. Perspectives come at me from public educators, researchers, and most importantly, an ever-growing network of everyday heroes who leave their jobs or other responsibilities to spend an hour every week—for months, even years—filling the holes that exist in at-risk children's hearts.

More than any other resource, however, our home serves as my most valuable research and development department. While my roles with the children's ministry and KIDS HOPE USA have provided me with a well-rounded, real-world view of children and childhood overall, Becky and I receive exhilarating learning opportunities daily, courtesy of our very own teenagers.

In an ideal world, the responsibility to teach this book's lessons belongs to parents. Today's world, though, falls short of ideal. When a parent is unable or unavailable, other adults must step in; someone must engage children in a deliberate manner and teach them how to navigate life. This book's primary voice addresses moms and dads, but I passionately hope its content will equip all adults who have the opportunity to speak into children's hearts.

Your Role

When I said that Becky and I receive "learning opportunities," that's exactly what I meant. Parenting mimics a class that never ends — always a new topic, constant tests, but no syllabus to point out what lies ahead. I fully expect that right at the moment I feel confident I know what I'm doing, our kids will leave home to strike out on their own. Please don't ask what grade I've earned thus far. Does effort count for extra credit?

Yet while you and I learn, we must also teach. A letter sent to parents of newborns in Miami-Dade County hospitals speaks clearly about this critical role: "Keep in mind that you are, and will always be, your child's first and most important teacher."[3] Instead of feeling weighed down by the implied responsibility of that message, picture a teacher. If you look closely at his or her desk, you'll see a lesson plan. You now have one in your hands, too. And class is in session.

Will childhood years magically make sense and become happier for your son or daughter overnight? Unlikely — valuable education rarely works that way. As with every task, though, at some point it's time to just jump in and get started.

That time arrives when you turn this page.

> "For gaining wisdom and instruction;
>   for understanding words of insight;
> for receiving instruction in prudent behavior,
>   doing what is right and just and fair;
> for giving prudence to those who are simple,
>   knowledge and discretion to the young ...
> Listen, my son, to your father's instruction
>   and do not forsake your mother's teaching."
>
> *Proverbs 1:2 – 4, 8*

Questions for Reflection or Discussion

1. What key lessons did you learn as a child that shape your character today?
2. Picture teenagers or young adults that you respect and admire. What characteristics do they exhibit?

BELIEVE THAT YOU MATTER / LIVE LIKE OTHERS MATTER MORE

Self-trust is the first secret of success.
RALPH WALDO EMERSON[1]

Believe That You Matter

Ben played on a fifth- and sixth-grade basketball team I coached. For the first nine games of our season, Ben failed to score. Actually, nobody recalled him even attempting a shot. He seemed content to simply watch as the game took place all around him. Why did Ben bother to play?

His mom faithfully brought him to every practice and dropped him off for games. She never stayed, though. Probably too busy. Maybe she realized her son only played because every player rotated in — that was a league rule. On offense, we hoped he would just stay out of the way. On defense, I encouraged him to get *in* an opponent's way — and I cheered him on when he did. That was the only thing I could find to cheer about for Ben. And for nine games I looked hard.

Game ten, everything changed.

As we did each week, our team met before the game in a hall outside the gym. Our last game held big stakes; a victory meant a winning season. That's not supposed to matter to players, but it mattered to the coach. Ben continued his tradition of arriving last. But this week he walked in with his mom and a friend.

Ben proudly introduced me to his out-of-town guest. His best friend, he said. I smiled and said hello. Inside, though, I cringed, picturing the ridicule Ben would endure after his buddy watched him play. His mom decided to stay and watch too. So I casually said to Ben and his cheering section, "We really need you today."

He took me seriously.

Our opponents had decided they could leave Ben open and use his man to double-team our key player. They figured wrong. Midway through the third quarter, the ball came to Ben only a few feet from the basket. The defense paid no attention. After a pause to build his confidence, Ben took his first shot of the season—and scored!

I called time-out so we could celebrate this monumental moment, and to let Ben relish the cheers. When play resumed, our team stole the ball, and somehow Ben caught another pass in the same position. With no hesitation, he shot and scored again. I felt so much joy that I again cupped my hands and trumpeted, "Time-out!" My fist triumphantly pumped the air. "This is why I coach!" I told the referee.

Two possessions later, Ben hit another shot. The referee pleaded with me not to further delay the game with another time-out. But I couldn't have done that anyway, because I stood there speechless at the spectacle unfolding before me. For the first time all season, I left this unlikely superstar in for the entire half. By the end of the game, Ben had racked up twelve points—scoring on every shot he took, from a variety of distances and angles. He came through when we needed him; we won the game by ten points. The grander victory, though, belonged to Ben.

"What happened?" I asked Ben.

"My friend and my mom came to my game," he said.

Translation: *For the first time this season, people cared enough to watch me. I believed that I mattered to someone. So I played with confidence. I believed in myself.*

I like to think we might have gone undefeated that season if his mom had attended the first nine games. Don't tell her, though; that only matters to the coach. Besides, Ben's season—and especially his last game—reveals the truth behind this chapter's first lesson: Kids need to believe that they matter.

Time-out.

Many years ago, experts began stressing the need for kids to walk through life fueled by belief in a high-achieving self. Children raised in this way grew up and did enjoy success, so that approach seemed appropriate. Then the next generation arrived and began to under-achieve compared to their parents, which created a problem. When accomplishments fell short of expectations, authentic praise proved difficult to share. As a result, moms and dads over-compensated and injected children with frequent shots of contrived self-esteem to artificially build them up. More recently, a fresh wave of advice now drenches those same parents with guilt because they have created a generation of narcissistic children. We're told that kids now possess entitlement-hungry egos-on-steroids. The expert opinion pendulum appears poised for a full return swing.

> Are not two sparrows sold for a penny? Yet not one of them will fall to the ground outside your Father's care. And even the very hairs of your head are all numbered. So don't be afraid; you are worth more than many sparrows. (Matthew 10:29–31)

Is either extreme appropriate? Let's look for an optimum mid-point where kids believe they matter (because they do) at a healthy level. In the following pages, we'll take a look at some of the best ways to affirm a child's worth. Later, this chapter's counterpart lesson will deliver the key elements necessary to ensure that kids stay at such a level—and that they learn to value others as well.

As we consider why it's important to affirm kids, reality is the best place to start. Regardless of age, socioeconomic conditions, or popularity, confident kids engage life. Conversely, a girl who wakes up every morning unsure if she matters to anyone, including herself, will eventually conclude that she doesn't—and that will be followed by doubts about the value of school, church, and family. Unfortunately, a growing number of kids lack an adult in their lives who lets them know that they matter at all.

Kids like Robert. Too many children share his story—broken family, dysfunctional neighborhood, splintered spirits, life out of order. In third grade, his principal believed life had overwhelmed this young boy and that he stood little chance to graduate, even from elementary school. Her opinion came with good reason; Robert couldn't read. Studies show that children who fall behind academically after first grade stand little chance of catching up unless extraordinary effort takes place on their behalf.

Then everything changed.

Robert began to meet with Ron, a mentor from a nearby church's KIDS HOPE USA program. For just an hour a week, Robert met with Ron in his school's library. They talked. They laughed. They read together. For the first time in his young life, Robert enjoyed an adult's attention and affirming words. The extraordinary happened. As a result, Robert realized that he mattered to Ron. Finally, Robert had a reason to believe he mattered.

Fast-forward to fifth grade. Ron still shows up every week, and Robert's principal now believes he'll graduate—from high school. Her conviction comes with good reason; he's now a great reader. "What happened with Robert," she says, "is a miracle."

Ron sidesteps personal credit. "I just kept telling him I believed in him," he says, "and all of a sudden he could read after all."

Reading matters. School matters. Life matters. But only after a child believes *he* matters. How will a child embrace this truth if no one shares it with him?

Because you're reading this book, it is clear that your children do have someone willing to teach them the lesson "Believe That You Matter." They have you to convince them of their worth. Please take your role seriously by avoiding the temptation to oversimplify this lesson's importance. In today's world in which parents push children toward overachievement, your daughter might believe she matters, but only if she _____. (You fill in the blank; common choices would include stays thin and attractive, earns high grades, displays exceptional talent in sports or arts, or behaves inside narrow expectations.) Don't let that happen.

Fortunately for the 99 percent of us who fall short of those descriptors, looks and achievement and behavior don't equal worth. But as parents, that truth doesn't relieve us of our duty. Self-worth (self-perception, self-value, self-esteem, self-regard — whatever you want to call it) in appropriate measures will supply a child with the essential confidence to engage life and believe that life matters. And parents are the best source for measured doses of exactly that.

Hall of Fame football great Mike Singletary blitzed through the NFL for several years as one of the most feared, successful, and confident linebackers to ever play the game, and now he coaches a team. He knows the value of a healthy self. In his book, *Daddy's Home at Last*, he says, "For your children to have self-esteem, they must first respect themselves and judge themselves to be worthy. They must develop an appreciation for their specialness and uniqueness. Where do they acquire such feelings of self-regard in the first place? You can't buy self-respect at the corner drug store or at the outlet mall. You learn that attitude from concerned, loving parents."[2]

Well said, coach.

To help your children grow up with confidence, let's look at how you can teach them they matter. Every teen in our focus group who said his or her parents taught this lesson described different approaches their parents took. The moms and dads in our focus groups shared a variety of ideas too. Fortunately, all fall within three easy-to-remember categories: words, actions, and time.

Words

"Here's how I know I matter to my mom," one teen explained. "Lots of mornings I wake up and see 'You are beautiful the way you are' written on my mirror."

Simple words. Personal words. Words often repeated. Shared mouth to ear or on the mirror, your words will provide steady answers to the question "Do I matter?" that constantly floats through your child's mind. Focus-group parent Brian provides a unique perspective on how he knows words work well. "My wife often puts notes in our kids' lunches to remind them of how much they're valued. Other kids notice and will, occasionally, ask them if they have 'one of those notes.'"

> So God created mankind in his own image, in the image of God he created them; male and female he created them.... God saw all that he had made, and it was very good.
> (Genesis 1:27, 31)

Lunch mates would likely trade their Doritos or their dessert for "one of those notes." Why? Because every kid hungers for such words. And this appetite knows no age limit. Just ask Laurie. "When our kids were ages eight and five, I bought a journal for each of them and started writing letters in each book that shared my affection, my feelings, my love," she says. "As they struggled in their teen years, we would pull the journals out and read the letters. The words reminded them of how much they mean to my husband and me. We were going to wait until they were older to show them the journals, but they *really* needed to hear those words as teenagers."

Simple words will accomplish plenty. According to a focus-group teen, "My parents let me know that I matter because they always tell me they love me."

Actions

Words have their limits, though, as articulated in a quote commonly attributed to Andrew Carnegie: "As I grow older, I pay less attention to what men say. I just watch what they do."

One need not be a business tycoon to see the value that actions possess. A focus-group teen shared a simple picture of success: "My parents help me believe that I matter when they always make big deals about my birthdays and other times during the year."

Simple, yet deliberate acts. Try too hard or too big and your kid will roll his or her eyes and wonder what parenting book you read. Little or no effort, though, yields proportionate results. So let's find the sweet spot using the teen's suggestion.

"We have a 'You Are Special' red plate that we use for birthdays, special occasions, and accomplishments," says Wanda, a mother of three. "Even as our kids grew older, they looked forward to that plate. Our daughter's fiancé didn't grow up with any traditions like this, and he often says that he wishes he had."

Imagine the sense of excitement in her family when the red plate appeared. For the fortunate recipient, what a thrill to receive reasons to legitimately believe "you noticed me—someone cares—yes, I matter." As the honest fiancé admitted, most people long to feel this way.

Even your everyday dishes can teach kids plenty. In fact, dishes perfectly represent your first parental action item: Do whatever it takes to eat meals together. Work hard at fitting them into your schedule.

Here's why. Study after study shows the direct benefits to children from family meals. Research verifies that "the more often families eat together, the less likely kids are to smoke, drink, do drugs, get depressed, develop eating disorders and consider suicide, and the more likely they are to do well in school, delay having sex, eat their vegetables, learn big words and know which fork to use."[3]

The same research concludes that a majority of teens who ate three or fewer meals a week with their families wished they did so more often. And further study showed that 65 percent of youth would give up a weeknight activity if it meant they could have a meal with family. Your kids want to eat with you, so leave work to get home in time for dinner. Take a pass on early evening activities. Say no to others so you can say yes to sitting around your own table, a choice that announces to children, "Having dinner with you matters because you matter."

When weeknight meals don't happen, prioritize weekend meals (or vice versa). Is your schedule still choking you? Try breakfast; just avoid inhaling your food, turning on the television, or any manner of multitasking. A chat can happen over Cheerios as easily as meatloaf. As long as you spend relaxed and extended time with your children, the food makes little difference.

Regardless of the menu, meals create unique opportunities to interact—but only with deliberate effort. So take turns recapping the day. Ask for highlights. Describe funny moments. Share challenges. Why? Researchers from the National Center on Addiction and Substance Abuse report that when asked the best time to talk to their parents about something important to them, nearly half of teens agree that during or after dinner is best.[4]

A focus-group teen articulates why mealtime discussions deserve more than leftover attention: "My parents make me feel like I matter by listening to what I have to say."

Although a simple act, some parents lack this profoundly important skill. Andrew's mom and stepdad quickly tire when listening to their second-grader, who accumulates so many words and thoughts throughout his day that he feels ready to burst until he shares them at home. Or tries to share them. After a sentence or two, they've learned how to effectively plug his flow—unaware of how this suffocates his spirit. "Nobody cares" is the message he's now accustomed to thinking on the way to his room.

Yes, actions speak louder than words. And there is no action that says "you matter" better than listening. Ask Andrew; he'd love to tell you.

Time

While words work well and actions prove that parents care, the most important approach requires your most valuable asset. A focus-group student said it best: "My parents spent one-on-one time with me and my siblings. This showed us that each of us is special and that we matter."

Start with attentiveness at bedtimes and mealtimes as the minimum time investments, especially with young kids. Then engage in joint activities—educational, recreational, whatever the purpose. Big payoffs result when, as children grow older and show interest in activities outside of home, you still maintain a high interest level.

Active, deliberate interest is required. In doing this, you'll demonstrate to your child that his or her desires matter enough to be noticed. Conversely, it's nearly impossible for a child to believe her desires matter when she consistently lands low on a parent's priority list.

For example, my son spent a long freshman football season as a rarely used backup player. While his confidence bobbed up and down like a trawler on rough seas, his perception of self-worth never sank because his mom and I made time to attend every game.

He knew why we sat in the stands: he matters to us.

Now think about the message sent by parents who make little effort to find ways to attend their children's events, no matter what type—sports, music recitals, art shows, school activities, science fairs, the list could go on for pages. Intense work schedules and crazy calendars are realities for most people, especially single parents, but the effort to work through such challenges means plenty to a child.

While time in the stands watching an event is good, those moments you spend participating in an activity with your child accomplish even more. Especially when your child chooses the activity.

Last year, my daughter, Erin, expressed interest in learning to cook. Now she and my wife spend every Sunday preparing dinner together. Stir together knowledge of cooking and focused time to talk. The recipe is that simple. What can you do to spend time with your child in her activity? Volunteer as a coach or serve as an assistant. Go on that field trip. Play catch in the yard. Help with a science project. Read books together. Take an overnight trip. Go for a long bike ride. Or show up at school and take her to lunch. Do anything that involves investing your time in her.

When you do, your child will believe she matters.

• • •

The lesson "Believe That You Matter" alone, however, can invite self-absorption and usher in its own set of problems. Rachel knows firsthand. "We overpraised our son, even when he didn't do something great," she says. "The result is that he's overconfident and conceited."

Ouch!

Consider this: Children who think only of themselves, talk only about themselves, and care only for themselves, progress from cute to confident to cocky. Callous—even cruel—as adults, they continue to think, talk, and care only for themselves. They believe they matter, for sure. Left unchecked, however, they can believe that *only* they matter. Thus the need for a perspective primarily focused on other people, leaving no room for narcissism.

An essay available on the web titled "The Fear That I Don't Matter" articulates the valuable balance achieved when children (and adults) learn both lessons included in this chapter: "I believe it's just a basic human need to feel as though one's life has meaning and worth. And I've never felt more worthy or deserving of my life than when I've done something to impact the quality of life for another human being."[5]

Combine the lesson you just read with the one you will read next, and you will discover how to live according to a great command from the Bible: "Love your neighbor as yourself" (Mark 12:31). It's a discovery definitely worth passing along to your children.

Live Like Others Matter More

Albert Einstein receives credit for these words: "Only a life lived for others is worth living." Yet his wisdom remains only a catchy theory until we intentionally teach such a lesson to children. They believe and behave quite differently upon arrival, don't they?

A newborn cries because he wants something from you. An infant smiles when you've made him comfortable and happy. A toddler sees the world as his to play with and has absolutely no desire to share. Reality check: You likely know plenty of grown-ups who still possess these qualities. So let's start with a lesson every parent must learn: A child will rarely, on his own, stop thinking of himself and begin focusing on other people.

> Do nothing out of selfish ambition or vain conceit. Rather, in humility value others above yourselves. (Philippians 2:3)

Teaching him that lesson is *your* job.

To excel in this critical role requires the belief that a child who values others will become a person who engages life—and who life enthusiastically embraces back. The best path ahead for your child starts with selflessness. The payoff for your son or daughter is committed friends, teachers' admiration, and other people's respect.

A refreshingly self-aware focus-group student said, "I sometimes only think of myself. My mom reminds me that if I would just step away from my own problems, I could make our family a whole lot better."

Yes, those words came from a real teenager.

Other People Matter, So Notice Them

To start, help your children develop a habit of thinking past themselves and of noticing other people. This takes time and effort. Julie learned that she needed to recalibrate her sons and daughters nearly every day. "I often told my kids in the morning to look for someone they could help that day—especially new kids," she says. "I asked, 'What can you do to help them not feel so alone?' Then we'd celebrate that night for any way that they actually did that."

Imagine how the world would change if more children left home for school each morning toting that challenge in their backpacks. Kids can make an extraordinary difference in the lives and hearts of peers when they take simple steps to live like others matter. And when they do, it's no small change.

For example, Bart describes a simple choice his son Jeremy made that created a special moment for an unlikely girl. "Our son is a good athlete, so he tends to be selected captain for games in gym class," Bart says. "One day, Jeremy decided to pick a very nonathletic girl for his team—he picked her first."

To you and me, choosing sides for relays in phys. ed. might rate low on a scale of important events. But this somewhat trivial task can cause very real feelings to race through young hearts. When a child consistently finds herself picked last, no matter the activity, the selection process provides a moment of humiliation—no matter how often it occurs. She realizes that nobody notices her. She ranks lowest. She's not wanted.

That day, everything changed.

The first-round draft choice felt the shock of a long-shot Oscar winner and expressed her disbelief with, "You're picking me? No one ever picks me!"

Bart believes that his son came up with the idea, in part, from parental example. "Jeremy gave that girl the gift of feeling valued because he's seen Jan and I do the same for other people, especially those who don't feel like they're valued. This was his turn to do that."

To live like others matter more sometimes means making choices that might cost you the game in exchange for a chance to make someone else feel like a winner. With one selfless selection, a routine pick became a special moment for an unlikely girl, a right-hearted boy, and a proud papa who has coached his kids well.

How many parents really teach their children that winning isn't everything? Sure, those words make a great consolation talk to a child who just lost at something. Imagine if more children entered Little League, the science competition, or gym class feeling less pressure to always win—despite their overenthusiastic coach's attitude (see the story at start of the chapter!). It's easy to picture more fun for everyone.

Yes, allowing kids to compete is good—as long as they do it in combination with good guidance.

In a world where me-first attitudes seem to light the pathway to success, we owe it to our children to teach them the value of team play. And team play comes from an others-first attitude. I worked a brief stint for a professional football team. During that season, I observed two types of quarterbacks; those with a self-absorbed attitude, and those who showed they valued others on the team—especially their linemen. Guess which quarterback group seemed to get sacked the most?

One quarterback stood out from the rest, though, because he took the team's offensive line out for an expensive steak dinner following every game. He enjoyed more time than most quarterbacks to throw the ball, and eventually led his team to a Super Bowl victory. When I tried to interview this team leader after a victory, he encouraged me to talk with the linemen because, he said, "When they win, we win."

Somewhere along the way, he received golden guidance. I referred to this story often as my son navigated youth athletics. (Although when he started playing quarterback I used a version that described the linemen's meals as pizza, a budget-friendly alternative to steaks.)

Let's look at three examples of ways you can make the lesson "Live Like Others Matter More" meatier as you serve it to your kids.

Family Matters

Start by ensuring that your children value those closest to them. "Believing others matter must start with your own family," says Judy. "We messed up by allowing our kids, when they reached a certain age, to have the option of whether or not they would go to their siblings' events. If I could do it over, I'd have them always show up and cheer on their brother or sister to make sure they weren't always just focused on themselves."

A focus-group teen shares a picture of success: "The message to treat others in our family the way you want to be treated is a recurring theme in our home."

Remember Wanda, the mom whose family celebrates one another with the red "You Are Special" plate? In addition to showing the honoree that he or she has value, the plate also dishes up the opportunity for family members to focus on someone other than themselves. If you decide to try Wanda's approach or something similar, make sure you resist the temptation to dilute the honor by celebrating additional siblings at the same time so they don't feel "left out." For their own good, leave them out.

> So in everything, do to others what you would have them do to you, for this sums up the Law and the Prophets.
> (Matthew 7:12)

Once the idea that family matters becomes the norm in your home, then take the next step and include others. Mark, a dad of three boys, says, "We modeled that other people matter by constantly reinforcing that our boys' friends are always welcome in our home; we can care about and love them too."

More Than Money

In 1897, Mark Twain wrote these words of timeless truth: "Some men worship rank, some worship heroes, some worship power, some worship God, and over these ideals they dispute—but they all worship money."[6]

True then, true now.

Part of your challenge, then, is to help your child live like people matter more than money. But how? Show children that you manage your money—not the other way around.

Author James Robison provides valuable perspective, writing, "With every 'We can't afford that,' parents reinforce the idea that money—not parents—makes decisions."[7] Sure, parents must teach children how to budget and stick to a financial plan. You'll help kids avoid becoming cash-crazed creatures when you say, "We will do this" (or "We won't do this") because you say so, not because of your current spending ability. Keep money in a safe place on the decision-making hierarchy—meaning not at the top.

> No one can serve two masters. Either you will hate the one and love the other, or you will be devoted to the one and despise the other. You cannot serve both God and money. (Matthew 6:24)

A challenging thought, indeed. Especially considering that we live in a culture so obsessed with money that even the limit of affordability serves merely as a well-worn speed bump on the road to acquiring more. Along the way, money increases in importance and eventually overtakes people. If this was not true and money obsession did not cause such pervasive problems, then finances would not take such a heavy toll on marriages. Try googling the phrase "why couples fight" and read how many results list money as the top issue.

When money causes or contributes to relationship problems at home, it matters too much—because it matters more than people.

The manner with which you treat money in front of your children will make a lasting impression. Every family faces different economic conditions, so you'll need to determine how it works best in your home. At risk of trivializing this issue, expert advice seems to focus on three aspects of wise money management: Spend less than you earn, regularly save, and generously give. (The next chapter covers generosity in more detail.) Model these three principles well, and money will not add up as more important than people.

When people matter more than money, a picture develops that every parent longs to see. When asked how parents taught their children to live for others, most teens in our teen focus group responded the way this student did: "My parents taught me to be unselfish by being unselfish themselves."

Twelve-year-old Carter serves as a great example of a boy who combines a healthy view of money and unselfishness. Instead of birthday gifts, he asked friends to give money to a ministry that had helped Carter and provided him a life-changing relationship with a caring adult. The day after his party, this young philanthropist gratefully gave $35 to the organization and expressed a desire for the funds to go toward finding more adults who will befriend kids.

Do people matter more than money to your kids? They do to Carter.

More Than Being Right

Reflecting on his life, television personality Hugh Downs once said, "Along the way I learned that it was not necessary to be triumphant over others to have a successful life."[8]

To live like others matter more than you do means learning to give up the need to always win the day. This starts with the universal desire to be right. A child who believes he or she is right all the time will grow up to be a lonely person.

The logic behind this lesson stands simple and stark. To start, if I'm right all the time, then I feel no need for your opinion. "I really don't care what you think" is an attitude that sprays like acid on those around me. It discourages interaction, diminishes relationships, and encourages the notion that I rule a little kingdom. And oh, how easy that delusion becomes to believe, especially in parent-to-child interactions. Because parents are right all the time, or so we often think—and, unfortunately, act.

If my kids believe that I think I'm right all the time, then they'll eventually want to feel that way with others. I admit that I'm a work-in-progress on this issue. Let me offer an example.

Not long ago, our family returned from a vacation. During a layover before our last flight, we replenished our supply of snacks at an airport shop. My daughter finds that salty snacks help mitigate mild motion sickness, so we purchased a bottle of soda and a bag of Chex Mix. With only a few minutes remaining before the door closed for our flight, I hastily paid the cashier, grabbed the soda, and did a walk-run to catch my family.

Practice playing second fiddle. (Romans 12:10, *The Message*)

Five minutes into the flight, Erin's stomach began to wobble, so she asked for the soda. No problem; I handed it to her. Then she asked for the Chex Mix. Problem. No one could find our salty snack.

A discussion took place after our frantic search. We traced the problem back to the counter. Who left the Chex Mix at the store? That's the question I kept asking. Yes, I paid the cashier. Yes, I grabbed the soda. Yes, I should have taken both items. But for some reason—one that might require counseling—I couldn't confess to the crime of leaving the snack behind. Fortunately, the soda helped my daughter. So we dropped it and forgot the issue. Or so I thought.

This afternoon I asked my son and daughter if they could possibly search deep in their memories to a time when I acted like I thought I was right. After a few moments of hearty, sincere laughter, they both exhaled the words "Chex Mix!"

"Sometimes you come across as thinking you're right all the time because you can't admit that you're wrong," said Scott.

I can't be right all the time if I admit when I'm wrong. Please join me as I resist the urge to simply teach this concept and work, instead, to model it.

Caution: You Can Go Too Far

As with any lesson, it's possible to take this concept further than intended. At times, deliberate consideration of this book's lessons may invite an unwitting overdose. Janet, who leads a ministry for her church, provides a glimpse into her realization that she had gone too far: "Although we wanted to teach our children the lesson that others matter more by our example, I went overboard by not putting boundaries on myself," she said. "The result is that my son believes that I think others matter more than he does to me because I stayed so busy serving other people in my ministry."

Well said, Janet. She seems to have no problem admitting her mistake and realizing that while putting others first, we must place family first of all. I can learn a lot from her example as I try to teach my own children this valuable lesson.

QUESTIONS FOR REFLECTION OR DISCUSSION

1. Who made you feel like you were fearfully and wonderfully made as you grew up? What did they do that made you feel this way?

2. What main point did Jesus share about our worth in Matthew 10:29 – 31? Why does he mention to not be afraid?

3. List specific messages you send to your children to help them believe they matter. Ask others to develop similar lists, then compare and share ideas.

Appreciate Those Who Serve You / Make Serving Others a Priority

Daddy taught us by words and example that service is the
rent we pay for living, the very purpose of life and not
something you do in your spare time.
Marian Wright Edelman[1]

Appreciate Those Who Serve You

A young African man named Jimmy held the disbelieving attention
of the crowd when he spoke at a conference for young American church
leaders. During a testimonial for an international aid organization, he
described the extreme conditions of his everyday life. He detailed the
daily struggle to survive. "But then," he said, "a new day arrived."

When Jimmy was eight years old, a person halfway around the
globe decided to sponsor him, which meant he could eat, enjoy shelter, and attend school. He began a fresh journey in life, made possible through financial support from someone he knew only through
occasional letters. This journey helped Jimmy complete his education
and start a career—a future few people in his land dare to dream.
Now, he was sharing his nineteen-year journey to encourage others
to become sponsors.

Then, in front of thousands, came an amazing moment.

The conference host asked Jimmy if he'd ever talked with Mark, his sponsor. He had not. The host asked if he wanted to meet Mark. Before Jimmy could answer, Mark walked across the stage toward him. Although they'd never met, the two embraced one another as best friends. And the previously articulate Jimmy could say nothing; he dropped to his knees and wept with pure gratitude.[2]

This young man from across the ocean set a high-water mark for appreciation.

Anyone with experience working with kids knows that even a small fraction of Jimmy's thankfulness would be a huge step forward for many children. Although parents want their sons and daughters to possess attitudes of gratitude, too many youngsters lack basic skills in expressing appreciation. This is a problem worth solving.

Children adept at offering timely and authentic thanks demonstrate rich character and along the way exude an almost magnetic charm. It is not surprising that people prefer to engage with kids who freely recognize and appreciate efforts made on their behalf, especially when compared with children straitjacketed by self-entitlement. Picture your family: Which description applies to the children you see?

Without clear guidance, most children don't express appreciation for people who serve them—those who provide for their basic needs, orchestrate fun experiences, help them learn, give them a gift, or make lunch.

A television news team from Minneapolis-St. Paul provided evidence of this reality. Anchor Amelia Santaniello of WCCO-TV found a middle school willing to let her serve incognito as a lunch worker. She served chicken tenders to students, intentionally making eye contact and saying, "There you go," to encourage interaction. Ms. Santaniello kept a running count of the students who expressed thanks as she served them.

"In the end, 42 percent of the kids during the first lunch period said the 'magic words,'" Santaniello reported. "They actually outperformed the grown-ups. Of the six adults I served, only a couple said thank you." Later, she asked a few students who said thank you why they did so while others did not. One boy said, "Well, I guess it's just how I was raised."[3]

Good guess.

Every birthday, Christmas, or any other time our children receive a gift, my wife encourages Scott and Erin to write thank-you notes. Full disclosure: Becky gives them a no-choice directive, because we both believe this is a skill that kids will fail to develop independent of strong guidance. Schools don't teach thankfulness; but then, schools aren't responsible for raising our children. Nor is the children's ministry at church, which primarily points thankful hearts toward heaven while playing a supplemental role to parents in nurturing kids toward maturity.

If our kids can't express their appreciation, people will eventually believe that they aren't appreciative.

Becky knows that true appreciation must result in action. She passionately insists that our children grow up to routinely express appreciation; they will treat it as if it's as normal as brushing teeth. If they can organize and express specific thoughts on paper, they'll more effectively articulate hearty thanks on the phone and in person. To jot a simple note on kid-friendly stationery within a forty-eight-hour response window requires little investment by you or your child. But other people will feel great about whatever kind

> One of them, when he saw he was healed, came back, praising God in a loud voice. He threw himself at Jesus' feet and thanked him—and he was a Samaritan. Jesus asked, "Were not all ten cleansed? Where are the other nine? Has no one returned to give praise to God except this foreigner?" Then he said to him, "Rise and go; your faith has made you well." (Luke 17:15–19)

act they performed, and your child will develop valuable, life-long thanking skills.

That's what happens when children learn to appreciate those who serve them.

Becky's approach is simple and worth mimicking: Feel grateful, say thanks, and show appreciation.

Feel Grateful

Every October 31, inauthentic gratitude haunts most American homes. The doorbell rings, voices shout "trick or treat," and hands grab for little candy packages. Some goblins will say thank you; their words muttered over their shoulders as they run to the next house. No doubt the number of kids who express any gratitude while facing the door lands far south of half; it likely flies below the lunch-lady study results.

The trick to changing habits for one night is to help children learn to *feel* appreciation the other 364 days of the year. The road to that end starts with helping kids notice other people's efforts.

Jerry provides a practical example of how he steered his two sons in this direction. "When they were young, my boys struggled with the coaching they received in sports," he says. "So I would ask them what they could learn from the coaches — rather than just letting them vent. This helped the boys value and appreciate their coaches."

Life comes at children fast because so many experiences are completely new to them. Just like a guide on a tour bus, make it your role to point out important sights for kids to notice. The coach, the teacher, the waitress, the crossing guard, the bus driver, a generous grandparent, even a sister — constantly draw attention to these people and their acts of service. Then watch your son's ability to feel appreciation grow.

And this important first step of appreciating those who serve him *will* grow. Author Bill Robinson, in his book *Incarnate Leadership*, describes a father-son trip to a local racetrack when he was eleven. Now a university president, he still remembers how his dad had little or no interest in racing, would likely have preferred to spend time elsewhere, but still selflessly treated young Bill to an evening of roaring motors and junk food. He also can vividly recall the moment he looked at his dad and thought, "He gave up something to give me worth."[4]

Yes, children can feel authentic appreciation, but only after you teach them to notice the people who serve — or sacrifice — for them.

Say Thanks

There is no doubt that the words "thank you" lift the spirits of those who hear them. But what difference do those two words make on the sender? A *New York Daily News* article reports "Teaching your kids to say 'thank you' can actually be good for their health."

Reporter Eloise Parker shares information from a study by psychologists at the University of California and the University of Miami that concludes, "Youngsters who took part in daily gratitude exercises reported higher levels of alertness, enthusiasm, determination, attentiveness and energy."[5]

Parents typically force children to eat vegetables for those same benefits!

Along with healthy eating habits, healthy thanking habits should start early. From the day her first child arrived, Laurie and her husband took every opportunity they could to overtly model and encourage saying "please" and "thank you." Then, similar to Jerry's earlier comments, they used athletic league settings to build something greater than wins and losses. "We taught our kids, starting when they were quite young, to thank their coaches after every practice and every game," she says. "Sometimes, coaches didn't know what to say and looked at them weird, so we also had to teach them to be prepared for any reaction."

Focus-group parents agreed that children learn to express thanks based more on what they see than on what you say.

Kevin saw this truth lived out with his children. "We taught our kids from an early age to show honor and respect to adults," he says. "My wife and I showed them how by frequently going up to people in uniform (police, firefighters, military) and saying, 'Thank you for serving us.' On a recent family trip, my son took the initiative to approach a soldier in an airport and thank him—just like he'd watched us do for years.

"The officer came over to where we were standing. With a tear in his eye, he shared that he had recently lost his own son. To have our boy thank him touched his heart in a way he desperately needed."

Watch how often you hear your child express appreciation for someone who's done something for her. If she doesn't say thank you when you're nearby, assume that she doesn't when you're nowhere close. Then self-examine your own habits in the gratitude department. She learns to say thank you through the example you provide. Do you thank the person who hands you chicken nuggets in the drive-through?

Show Appreciation

The first time my daughter poured a drink into her small plastic cup, she stopped too late. As we both looked at the lemonade puddle on the counter, she said, "Guess the cup doesn't hold enough."

"Overflow with thankfulness," says Colossians 2:7. Let appreciation pour out, puddle up, and soak the people around you. The best place to start? At home.

"We were very direct at encouraging our kids to appreciate one another, thank each other, serve each other, and to do things for one another," says Jackie. "If they can't do this with their own brothers and sisters, how can we expect them to do it for others?"

Warning: Effort required.

Siblings must work hard to appreciate one another instead of taking one another for granted. And parents must tirelessly monitor family dynamics. Kate, a mother of four, knows this well and described a prolonged experience in her family: "My youngest daughter is very sensitive and hurt easily. I took our other three children aside one day and said we needed to work on loving her better. Then we started holding a weekly family discussion about how we're doing at loving each other. In those meetings, we all agreed to not make fun of one another, especially in public."

Does every member of your family appreciate the others, or does ridicule rule the day? The latter option stands as the honest answer in way too many families.

> So then, just as you received Christ Jesus as Lord, continue to live your lives in him, rooted and built up in him, strengthened in the faith as you were taught, and *overflowing with thankfulness.* (Colossians 2:6 – 7, emphasis added)

Again, actions will pack more influence than words—and Trisha knows this firsthand. "My husband has always insisted that after I fix a meal, I must leave the kitchen cleanup duties to him," she says. "Our kids definitely paid attention to his example.

"One night recently, when my husband was away on business, I began to clear the table after dinner. Our youngest son asked me, 'What are you doing?' He made me leave the kitchen so he and the other kids could take over."

Does this make mom feel appreciated? Based on the glow of Trisha's face as she told this story, I'd say yes.

To authentically show appreciation—to overflow with thankfulness—requires action above expectations. A family that says "Thanks for dinner, Mom" exhibits good manners. But "We appreciate you so much we'll do the dirty work" shows appreciation that will light up a mom's heart.

Write a note, notice a coach's efforts, say thank you, load the dishwasher—all of these relatively easy tasks exceed today's common expectations. And every day, such responses inch closer to extinction in our culture of self-entitlement and me-centricity.

Fortunately, parents can easily take these and other acts of appreciation off the endangered species list through consistent modeling and positive reinforcement. Imagine what happens in a young heart when a parent says, "I heard you say thank you to the bus driver today. Way to go! In that moment you probably made her day—because you definitely made mine!"

Your child will stand out from the crowd when she appreciates anyone who serves her. Help her see these moments of opportunity as moments well spent.

. . .

Darlene, a mother of four, is puzzled. "Our two sons went on a youth trip," she says. "During the event, one son gave all his money away during a special offering to help the poor. But on the long bus ride home, my other son would not even give his own brother a dollar for a hamburger. How can two boys from the same family, with the same experiences, act so differently?"

For countless reasons, even a well-mannered child—like Darlene's miserly son—can grow comfortable with being served. Too comfortable. So comfortable, in fact, that he remains a perpetual recipient and never the servant.

To counter such temptation may have been essayist Deirdre Sullivan's inspiration when she wrote, "Most days my battle is doing good versus doing nothing."[6]

Effort anemia afflicts many of today's kids, with symptoms that include the inclination to do as little as possible for others (preferably nothing) and to worry only about one's own needs. Left unchecked, what starts as self-sufficiency can become self-centeredness.

The antidote: action. Do something for another person. The next lesson will help children victoriously fight the battle of doing good versus doing nothing.

Make Serving Others a Priority

The first three words of the Golden Rule found in Matthew 7, "Do unto others," describe a critical step in transforming a person from a consumer to a contributor. Indeed, for a child to develop compassion for the world around her, she must have an ability and a willingness to actively look for opportunities to meet others' needs—and then to take action. The secret to helping her achieve success? Constant encouragement. At first, a child will believe that serving someone else feels good. Eventually, it becomes a normal feeling—even a great habit!

But habits never develop overnight.

A focus-group teenager describes what deliberate and successful parental encouragement can look like. "One time when I was in fifth grade, everyone in our family seemed to be in a bad mood," she said. "So my mom told all of us to find someone to serve that day.

"Even though this girl at school bothered me a lot that particular day, I remembered my mom's coaching and offered to take the girl's backpack and hang it up on her hook. This act is a pretty big deal in fifth grade. I remember the look on her face; she was so grateful and said that it made her day. I admit that it made mine too!"

Maybe you've heard the sage adage that a man never stands as tall as when he kneels to help a child. In similar fashion, no one stands taller than a child who selflessly helps those around her. But kids need a boost to get that practice underway. They'll find firm footing when they step up in the three basic areas of selfless servanthood: time, talent, and treasure.

Time

To make serving others a priority requires a child to learn that time spent helping someone else is time well invested. Often, such opportunities require mere moments, not many hours. A child's receptivity to bite-sized chances provides a preview to the overall lend-a-hand attitude she can one day possess.

Start by encouraging children to offer simple assistance on quick, little tasks around the home. How? First show; then tell. Prior to barking, "Go help your mother," I must consistently demonstrate my willingness to set aside what I'm doing and step up to help. (My wife's favorite sentence in this book.) Only when my kids see me walk away from the computer, television, or whatever activity to lend assistance will they begin to believe serving others is a priority for everyone, not just a lazy dad's directive. With my actions a comfortable distance in front of my words, I can then move on to "C'mon, let's go help Mom."

Once serving one another routinely happens at home, expand the lesson to other settings. Again, start with showing before telling. "My wife volunteers a lot at school, and our kids see her," says Steve. "She models well."

Then Steve goes on to describe a logical next step: "Our family small group volunteers at nursing homes and food pantries together. It's a great way to teach our kids that serving others is important."

Important enough to appear on the calendar. Important enough to preempt other activities that these families could pursue. Important enough to deserve a portion of a family's most precious commodity: time.

Along the way, Steve's children most certainly are learning an important lesson. Educators everywhere agree that a child retains only a small portion of what's said, slightly more of what they see, and significantly greater portions of what they do.

Darlene describes the key element that unlocks any family's ability to teach their children to serve others: "We always made it a priority to take our kids with us when we served in local mission organizations," she says. "That way, they could not only see us at work helping, but they could also join in with the work."

Everyone receives twenty-four hours in a day, and at least some discretion over their use of that time. A child who sees, hears, and experiences how to prioritize meeting others' needs will live into the words of Galatians 5:13: "You, my brothers and sisters, were called to be free. But do not use your freedom to indulge the flesh; rather, serve one another humbly in love."

> Be devoted to one another in love. Honor one another above yourselves. (Romans 12:10)

Talent

Many churches teach about spiritual giftedness — identifying unique abilities given by God and showing how to use them within a local congregation. Those gifted with the ability to lead should lead. Those who can teach should teach. Singers should sing. Artists should create. And the list goes on.

Talent, as we'll use it in this lesson, exists as a broader brushstroke. Maybe you possess high aptitude to do something that serves others. Great. Do it. More frequently, though, meeting needs will require less giftedness and more availability. Therefore, let's consider talent as any action you can take to get something done for someone else.

To put it another way, we'll call talent *effort*. An example may help.

While my daughter and I drove on a busy nearby highway, we came to an abrupt stop behind a car that stood still near a heavily traveled intersection. Traffic moved too fast beside us for me to change lanes. A moment later, the young driver opened her door and stood outside her car looking very scared. Her hazard lights flashed, but dimly. "This is dangerous," I said to Erin as I activated my flashers and opened my door.

"Will your car start?" I asked the frightened high school girl.

"No," she said, "and I don't know what to do."

"Get back in and I'll push you off the street," I told her.

A moment later, her car slowly crept off the road and out of harm's way. She followed my next advice and stayed in the driver's seat as she spoke on a cell phone to get assistance. In less than thirty seconds, I used a form of talent to help someone.

"Why did you do that?" Erin asked as we drove away.

"That girl needed someone to help her," I said, "and I was right there."

The High School Girl's Version of the Same Story

So my car just, like, quits right there near the stoplight on the highway. I'm standing next to my car, trying to call my dad and I see this black Jeep almost crash into me. Hello, my trouble flashers are on, dude. Then, OMG, the guy driving jumps out of his Jeep and runs up to me. I'm thinking "Great, a creeper coming to do something weird to me." He asks me if my car won't start. Hello again, I'm stopped in the middle of the road. So he tells me to get back in the car, which was a great idea rather than stand in the road with him and almost get hit by all the people with nothing else going on other than staring at us. I don't think he noticed me lock the door after I got in the car. But then he pushes my car so I'm out of all the traffic, which was pretty nice, I guess. He tells me to stay in my car and call someone, as if I planned to just listen to music. A few minutes later, my dad pulled up and took me home. I want a new car that works.

Do I possess a spiritual gift to move cars? Of course not. I do, though, have strong legs and enough body weight to push an auto. As did several able-bodied guys in cars stopped behind and beside us. Why did they stay in their comfortable air-conditioned cars and wish that I'd move faster? Maybe their parents never read this book.

While my back felt sore for just a few days, the lesson of using talent for someone else—in the form of simple effort—will stick with Erin for a long time. I suspect that a guy or two from the gallery may also remember this lesson and take action next time. Effort can, after all, be contagious.

I know that not everyone can shove cars down a street. (Although it's easier than it sounds, trust me.) But nearly all kids do possess valuable but unspectacular abilities that can serve others well. The real challenge for parents is to help their children deploy, rather than find, talent.

For instance, one mom in our church arranged with a local nursing home for middle school and high school students to volunteer there. Every kid knows how to play, so they organize and lead games like bowling with the residents. A few girls paint ladies' nails. All the while, they smile and laugh. Other youth have, at times, offered free babysitting for parents who could use a night out but have tight finances. Any child can handcraft a birthday card for a neighbor, rake leaves, or shovel snow.

Reality check: Few kids come up with these ideas on their own, so help them.

"My wife and I coached our kids to approach serving others in this way—figure out how to serve other people while doing things you enjoy," says Jarrett. "If you love to bake, then bake for other people. In other words, connect what you enjoy with serving other people."

To get started, though, keep it simple.

Mention the concept of feeding the hungry and our minds

typically race toward a soup kitchen or food pantry. Wonderful opportunities to serve, no doubt. But what about the lonely people on your street who are starved for companionship? "We consistently invite elderly people in the neighborhood over to our house for dinner," says Debbie. "At first, our kids complained. But now they like the experience of bringing joy into someone's life."

As you teach children that their efforts — big or small — can make a real difference, you will guide them down the path God wants them to travel: "Let us consider how we may spur one another on toward love and good deeds" (Hebrews 10:24).

> Suppose a brother or a sister is without clothes and daily food. If one of you says to them, "Go in peace; keep warm and well fed," but does nothing about their physical needs, what good is it?
> (James 2:15–16)

Treasure

In a society often correctly labeled materialistic, kids will either learn to serve others generously at home or they will likely not learn it at all. While a few philanthropic messages make their way into your mailbox or onto your television screens, they primarily (and wisely) seek to raise money — not teach lessons. Take away the tax benefit and what would happen to many donations? Compare the number of books focused on acquiring wealth with the number devoted to giving wealth away. While massive charitable acts make great headlines, like Bill Gates and Warren Buffet's challenge to fellow billionaires to give away at least half their wealth, your children will learn more from how *you* handle your treasure.

Generosity is more of an attitude than a dollar amount.

To start teaching children this lesson, consider that "treasure" includes more than just money; generosity also includes possessions.

Ben explains how this broader definition shapes the attitude of his home: "We have a family mission statement that includes our desire to be a family that serves others. One way we turn this desire into reality is by letting our neighbors use our pool anytime they want. They can come to our house anytime—our door is always open. In fact, we even give out our garage-door code so anyone can borrow what they need or go for a swim if we're not around."

Treasured possessions also exist in scales smaller than swimming pool-sized. "One year, we asked all the kids in our family small group to give up one of their stuffed animals or other favorite toys," says Steve. "Then they gave the toys to a local mission—with the belief that the toys could make someone else feel special."

Consider the highly memorable, hands-on lesson Steve and the other parents in his small group taught: their children learned to give away something they treasure instead of simply purchasing extra toys with mom and dad's cash.

As you help your children participate in generous acts, prepare for them to begin discovering and acting upon their own opportunities. "After school, I asked my son what he had for lunch, and he said 'nothing,'" says Danielle.

"I furrowed my brow and asked, 'Did Dad forget to give you lunch money?'" (Why do dads always receive the initial indictment?) "He went on to tell me that he gave all he had to a fundraiser at school to help kids in Haiti."

The choice facing Danielle at that moment became "Chastise him for unwisely giving away his lunch money and going without an important meal" or "Celebrate the generosity of his heart that's stronger than the hunger growling in his stomach."

She chose the latter. Don made a similar decision.

"Somehow, my son learned and believed the Bible verse that says, 'Good will come to those who are generous and lend freely'" (Psalm 112:5), says Don, "because he displays an amazing ability to give. For example, last Christmas his gift to me consisted of an envelope with cash and a note that explained how he knew how much a certain ministry meant to me, so he wanted me to use his money as a donation."

As the story continues, Don offers a peek at his teaching style.

"I told him that this might be the best Christmas gift I ever received. Why? Because in giving away this money (earned, by the way) with no material gain for either of us, he showed that he could give without anything in return, except for the satisfaction he felt in his heart. At the bottom of a note that expressed my appreciation, I wrote these words from Matthew 3:17, which says it best: 'This is my Son ... with him I am well pleased.' Love, Dad."

Affirmation acts as the most effective teaching tool at your disposal when it comes to building a heart of generosity in your child. Want your child to believe that good will come to him when he is generous and lends freely? Then notice and encourage him every time he serves others by sharing what he treasures.

A child who makes a priority out of giving away time, talent, and treasure will receive something much greater as a result. In his book *The Me I Want To Be*, John Ortberg writes, "If you can't do great things, Mother Teresa used to say, do little things with great love. If you can't do them with great love, do them with a little love. If you can't do them with a little love, do them anyway. Love grows when people serve."[7]

> Even in darkness light dawns for the upright,
>   for those who are gracious and compassionate and righteous.
> Good will come to those who are generous and lend freely,
>   who conduct their affairs with justice.
> Surely the righteous will never be shaken;
>   they will be remembered forever.
>
> *Psalm 112:4–6*

QUESTIONS FOR REFLECTION OR DISCUSSION

1. Rate your child on a scale of 1 to 10 based on how often he expresses appreciation: 1 (never) and 10 (constantly). Rating _____. Does that number need to change?

2. Describe the most recent time your child served someone else without your prompting. How will you spur her on as directed in Hebrews 10:24?

3. On a scale of 1 (never) to 10 (constantly), rate your child on her willingness to help others. Rating _____. How would other adults rate your child? Ask.

FORGET UNIMPORTANT STUFF / REMEMBER LIFE HAS CONSEQUENCES

Therefore do not worry about tomorrow, for tomorrow will worry about itself. Each day has enough trouble of its own.
MATTHEW 6:34

Forget Unimportant Stuff

Life brings challenges. Some are big and important. Others, though, deserve little fuss—or none at all. Often, the ability to enjoy life requires differentiation between the two, including the ability to avoid letting problems stay past their welcome. When children learn to identify and defuse nonserious issues, they are on course to walk a healthy path through life. Unfortunately, walking that path can feel more like tiptoeing through a minefield for children whose parents fail to teach them to forget unimportant stuff.

Many of today's kids live in a world of constant worry, fear, and anxiety over issues big and small. As a result, they wobble as they walk. *Time* magazine writer John Cloud confirms the quivers and shakes with evidence showing that anxieties and most phobias now typically begin to appear by age seven, that panic often appears by age ten, and that twenty percent of young people will experience depression at some point during adolescence.[1] Think of these facts as flashing mental-health-problem indicator lights, frantically signaling that something is very wrong.

So where does all this worry originate? Years of interaction with large numbers of kids has shown me that scared and anxious children are raised by scared and anxious parents.

The fact is, though, that much of the paranoia in the air is as unnecessary as it is heartbreaking. And ridiculous. A recent "Dear Abby" column endorsed a reader's suggestion that parents use a cell phone to take a photo of their child every day before he leaves the house.[2] The reason? To provide authorities with the most current picture available, including clothing, in case that child is abducted. This means that every day, a youngster will pose for a five-megapixel reminder of the incredible threats that wait just outside the front door. How many seeds of worry can a parent plant in a child's mind before constant worry becomes the norm?

Certainly, such crimes make our stomachs turn. But we must keep in mind that our society has sensationalized them to a deceptive degree.

Statistics show the chances that a stranger will abduct and kill a child stand as low as one in 1.5 million.[3] At the same time, the insurance industry estimates the odds of your home completely burning down are one in 16,000, and the likelihood of having your automobile totaled are one in 100.[4] The chances that a beloved pet's life will end is so high that tears might force you to stop reading—so let's skip it. Maybe your child should snap pics of your house, your car, and Sparky the dog before leaving for school—after all, greater odds exist that they'll disappear before he will.

Paranoid parents aren't the only culprits. Notice, in particular, how our country's free enterprise system has locked onto the scent of parental fear. Want your kids to feel petrified when it comes to outdoor adventures? Just tuck this new product under your arm as you head out for the day: a portable, wireless security system with sensors to place around your campsite, beach blankets, or picnic area. Anything that breaches this secure zone, from a wandering child to a hungry grizzly bear, causes alarms to sound and lights to flash. "The real value of the product is in child security," the inventor says. "You can easily create a perimeter at the playground, or the lake, or your campsite."[5]

When parents are encouraged to take when-you're-abducted pictures and to guard the perimeter, it's little wonder that kids fear the world in which they live. And it's a short step from there to developing hypersensitivity to anything in life that's unexpected. So much fuel exists to ignite anxiety, panic, and other disorders that kids begin feeling constantly anxious and panicky—and bear-hug any little problem so tightly they're unable to let go and move on.

But hope exists that parents can extinguish the unnecessary anguish. Data shows that even kids with a genetic disposition to anxiety, panic, and depression can persevere if they can learn to become resilient, which is the ability to forget the unimportant stuff, or at least to right-size it.[6] You will serve your child well when you help her develop this "inner perimeter."

Resilience guards a child from, literally, caring about every concern that wanders into her life—whether as unlikely as abduction by a stranger or as common as a friend's cruel comment. When a kid knows no better than to carry the weight of every issue, her capacity to embrace and enjoy life diminishes. Worry acts as a thief that steals joy, which is not the way God intended life to work.

> Who of you by worrying can add a single hour to his life?
> (Luke 12:25)
> Do not let your hearts be troubled and do not be afraid.
> (John 14:27)
> I have told you this so that my joy may be in you and that your joy may be complete. (John 15:11)

So do we blithely ignore all the challenges we face? I wish. Quick reality check: I have experienced the ups and downs of being a kid, an adventuresome youth, a parent of toddlers, a cancer patient, a children's ministry director, and currently a dad of two teenagers. An issue-free life doesn't exist. But with resilience, any person can enjoy life, whether young or older, even me.

With resilience, life can happen just as God intended.

You and I know that every child changes at her own pace as she grows — common knowledge that applies to this chapter's first lesson. Consider how a very young kid believes that *nothing* matters — spilling, letting daddy sleep, or a host of sanitary conditions — even though some things really do. On the other hand, way too many of our kids believe that *everything* matters — even though some things really don't.

> Anxiety weighs down the heart, but a kind word cheers it up.
> (Proverbs 12:25)

Let's look at four approaches we can take to help kids develop resilience that will guard them from reaching such a joy-robbing extreme.

Let's Talk

"When issues arose, I'd sit with my kids and let them talk it out," says Liz, a mother of three. "These chats helped them get through issues of all sizes because they had someone to confide in who would not try to solve their problems."

Liz's approach works wonders, according to many focus-group teens. "When I get stressed out over little things, like my homework or sports, either one of my parents will pull me aside and calm me down by talking with me," says one student. "They help me not get hung up over small details that I sometimes worry a lot about and forget about the unimportant stuff. Then I can move on. I'm glad they do that."

As children age, their maturity can fool parents into believing their kids don't want mom or dad's involvement. But consider how, at the same time that your daughter gives you a vibe to leave her alone, she's also facing very new, very real issues she's never encountered before—issues related to school, friends, sports, popularity, fitting in, clothes, homework—the list seems massive. Add hormones into the mix, if you dare, and you have a young person ready to discern alone the significance of whatever the world throws at her, right?

C'mon.

Scott Rubin, middle school pastor at Willow Creek Community Church in suburban Chicago, counsels parents to communicate with perseverance. "Even though your child might act like he doesn't want you to ask about his life, the opposite is true," Scott says. So keep trying.

You are in a better position than anyone else to help your child learn to distinguish between important and unimportant issues. Such discernment skills fail to develop when you fail to communicate. So ask often. Even when you receive little or no response, keep asking. When an issue sinks its teeth into your child, he'll appreciate knowing that you're available to talk it out.

Focus-group parents agree that one question serves as the most valuable tool to loosen the grip an issue has on a child. "In these discussions, I'd encourage my kids to talk through 'What's the worst that could happen here?'" says Winona. "Through these discussions, we'd usually figure out that the situation wasn't really so bad."

In addition to realizing that the worst-case scenario is not so awful after all, consider the assurance a child feels when he hears that he's normal and that other kids also deal with similar issues. Whatever message your child needs will arrive only when you talk together.

Remember, you will need to make the first move.

Laugh or Cry, Lighten Up, and Move On

"My daughter had to learn how to face people who would ask, 'Where's your dad?' after he had committed suicide," says Jean.

"Unfortunately, some people react quite strangely when we tell them what happened. So we developed a journal called *The Stupid Book*, in which we write the goofy responses we hear. No matter what she'd hear, she knew we would laugh about it as we recorded the comment, and then she could forget about it and move on."

Sometimes laughter is indeed the best medicine—as long as your child does the laughing first. I promise that if you snicker at the silliness of an issue as your daughter shares it with you, tears will reward your insensitivity. (Can you tell I learned this the hard way?) Instead, ask questions. Keep her talking. If she giggles, join in. It might, however, take a conversation or two to reach that point.

You've likely lived through many experiences that seemed traumatic at the time, but the memory of which now results in a chuckle—symbolically announcing, "I guess it wasn't all that bad." Laugh about your difficult memories with your children, and they'll see how you've learned not to take everything so seriously. Along the way, they'll figure out how to do the same.

At other times, the opposite side of the emotional spectrum needs expression. "When my son didn't make a sports team, I just had to spend time with him and let him cry," says Kim. "After letting his emotions drain, he saw it wasn't that big of a deal. I'm glad he didn't hold it in."

Laugh. Cry. Trust your instincts and picture yourself at his age. Along the way, make sure your input doesn't hinder progress. "I learned about all this way too late in parenting, which means I was too cold and too hard on our oldest child," says Norma. "I wish I would have done a better job teaching him that you can move on."

In Norma's defense, such a lesson looks different for every child and likely involves many swings and misses. I feel fortunate to have experienced an unexpected hit with this lesson.

In sixth grade my son, Scott, pitched for his Little League baseball team, and he threw extremely well. I possess little or no pitching skills, so I credit his talent to the head coach, Bill. In my role as assistant coach, I mostly cheered and carried equipment.

Partway through one game, though, Scott struggled. The more he threw, the worse he threw. I offered to give him a pep talk, and Bill agreed.

On the mound together, Scott told me he had no idea what was going wrong. "The more I try to figure this out, the worse I get," he said. "I've already walked three batters."

I could offer him nothing of value about his throwing motion. I didn't even try. Instead, I surprised both of us by sharing philosophical words that stuck: "The only pitch you have to worry about is your next pitch," I said. "Forget about what you've done, and think about what you need to do."

He struck out the next three batters. Bill wanted to promote me to pitching coach. I wisely declined and grabbed the equipment bag after the game.

According to Scott, that conversation has stayed with him ever since that summer day. Those words have proven helpful as he quarterbacks his high school team and perseveres through particularly tough school days. I hope he'll keep them his whole life as he faces whatever challenges life throws his way.

About Your Friends

Regardless of age, relationships matter. A lot. Only a fool would say that people fall into the category of unimportant stuff. In fact, social research shows that a person will know somewhere between three hundred and three thousand people throughout his or her lifetime.[7] (Such a volume of friends makes me glad our phone plan includes unlimited texting.)

While every relationship is a gift, a churn of new and different friendships is normal and necessary. What a relief for us parents who know that friendship issues can unnecessarily inflate well past what they deserve, and that, at times, they must burst for the good of everyone concerned. In others words, the world won't end over the need to find a different friend. A child will exercise that exact life skill over and over again. Maybe up to three thousand times.

"One day I came home from elementary school, and I was feeling sad because some kids were not being nice to me," a focus-group teen says. "As we talked about it, my parents suggested that I try to find the kids I *should* hang around with who *will* be nice."

"When my boys were in middle school, they had friends who rejected them. We had to continually remind them that it wasn't their fault, and that nothing was wrong with them," says Jay. "This helped them let go and move on."

> The righteous choose their friends carefully. (Proverbs 12:26)

Jay continues with more wise counsel: "To help children forget unimportant stuff often means helping them figure out who is important. They need help deciding whose opinion to listen to and whose opinion really doesn't matter. Kids hear all sorts of stuff that they need to filter. Of all the parenting that I tried to do well, I wish I would have done a better job at this."

Of course working out differences with friends is preferable to dumping them. However, kids also need to understand that people change and so will relationships. Fortunately, when a new friend enters the scene, your daughter will likely forget about the trauma and drama from whatever previous friendships went south.

This discussion requires a disclaimer. Parents must constantly discern that the issues their children face are, indeed, simply friendship issues and not bullying—a very real problem that requires much more than the lesson "Forget Unimportant Stuff" has to offer. Many excellent resources address this topic to the level of detail it deserves, with specific actions for parents and children to take. If you suspect that your child is being bullied—or is bullying someone else—immediately seek reliable advice.

A Line Exists

When you talk with your child about issues he faces, let him do the most talking. If you help him laugh or cry away a situation, make sure he does the laughing and crying. When he must right-size friendship issues or find new pals, help him make the decision—but don't take it upon yourself to prearrange a new buddy. If you tell your child how to feel, laugh, or cry about an issue, or you step into his or her friendship world, you may find your efforts counterproductive. It's way too easy for a parent to go too far in minimizing a child's concern or to add fuel that overdramatizes the situation. Perceived insensitivity might even make it worse.

"I learned to be careful not to dismiss some issues too quickly," says Jerry, "because what might not seem like a big deal to me could seem to be a very big deal to my child. This happened a lot when I'd give them a quick fix to their problem. I tried to help but messed things up."

Jody remembers a specific example. "Our son likes risky sports and broke his arm snowboarding. After six weeks, he had the cast removed. The doctor told him that he should wait another two weeks before getting back on the board. We acted like that was no big deal. But it was a really big deal to him. Some things that seem unimportant to adults will, in fact, be very important to children."

Great point, Jody. We serve children well when we resist the temptation to immediately share our opinions about what they face. Instead, discover how your child best processes issues—whether or not you take the same approach with your own junk.

Life contains plenty of content—some to keep; some to discard. To that end, the prophet Isaiah counsels us to take a light path through life: "Forget the former things; do not dwell on the past" (Isaiah 43:18).

A focus-group student offers wisdom about the benefit of following the prophet's words: "I learned that if you remember the unimportant stuff, you won't have room to remember the stuff that really *is* important."

> But one thing I do: Forgetting what is behind and straining toward what is ahead, I press on toward the goal to win the prize for which God has called me heavenward in Christ Jesus.
>
> *Philippians 3:13 – 14*

. . .

Numerous sources credit cinnamon as a tool to help regulate blood sugar. Many of the same reports warn that high amounts of the spice can prove toxic. Yes, too much of a good thing often produces unfortunate results.

While kids need to learn how to forget unimportant stuff, this lesson taken too far will deliver an unhealthy result—children who develop Teflon mentalities. They adopt an expectation that no problems or issues should stick to them. Soon, rules won't matter. One day, laws won't either.

Sound ridiculous?

Not likely, if you know children whose mom or dad always clean up after them. What begin as Lego messes may one day become legal messes. For children to have an accurate view of how life really works requires a complementary lesson.

Remember Life Has Consequences

"What's going to happen to me?"

Fear, like a 105° fever, blanketed me as I asked that question. Few memories from junior high school remain with me today. But this one sure does, including the perspiration and nausea.

Going in to eighth grade, I thought choir class only involved singing. I didn't realize that this class also required learning about music, reading notes, and other technical aspects. My voice couldn't carry a tune, and my mind struggled to understand how music works. While I couldn't fake a good voice, unfortunately I tried to fake the learning.

I cheated.

As I sat at a desk to take the first test, I fully realized how little I knew. So I glanced over at someone seated nearby and was amazed at how much he understood, how quickly and confidently he circled the correct answers, and how easily I could see his work.

Mrs. Mumaw, our music teacher, could just as easily see me. Midway through the test, she asked me to come forward and bring my test. "I'm not quite finished," I said, pretending to read a question and ponder the answer.

"Oh yes you are," she replied.

I knew what she meant, so I brought my test and placed it on her desk. In front of my peers, I tried to act as if nothing was wrong. Inside, though, my heart pounded at a prestissimo rate (musical terminology, in case you were wondering, for more than two hundred beats per minute).

After class, I tried to shake off what just happened. Forget the unimportant stuff, right? Then my buddy Dennis asked if I knew what would happen next. "Probably a lousy grade. But who cares? It's just music class, right?" I said.

Matt, another friend, overheard and said that he knew someone who received a failing grade for the whole semester for cheating. Chris added that he thought he knew someone expelled from school for the same reason, with the possibility of repeating the entire eighth grade—or being refused entrance to high school. When Dennis wondered whether the teacher calls the parents or if that task belongs to the principal, I stopped breathing.

Until that point, potential consequences had never entered my mind—almost as if I possessed immunity from any serious repercussions. Does your child feel ownership—personal responsibility—for her actions?

I decided to return to Mrs. Mumaw's classroom, apologize, and find out what fate awaited me. We talked about the bad choice I made and the options teachers have when a student cheats. She gave me an F on the test, which I clearly deserved. She offered to give me a low passing grade for the semester, but only if I studied, retook the test, and earned an A. And if I exhibited exemplary singing participation! Because I came back on my own and sincerely apologized, she felt these were sufficient consequences. For the remainder of that long semester, I studied hard and endured the ridicule of my buddies as I energetically—and loudly—sang.

While I still struggle to carry a tune and remember nothing about reading music, my choir class experience stuck with me. It was there, after all, that I learned a valuable lesson: Life has consequences. I must own responsibility for my actions. Choices really do matter.

> The upright give thought to their ways.
> (Proverbs 21:29)

The Bible addresses our need to consider the impact of our decisions: "This day I call the heavens and the earth as witnesses against you that I have set before you life and death, blessings and curses. Now choose life" (Deuteronomy 30:19).

Had Mrs. Mumaw not caught me, I might have scored well on that test. I might have adopted an attitude that viewed cheating as a legitimate option. Then it would have become an attractive option—in eighth grade, high school, college, my career, even with my taxes, maybe worse. Although the temptation to let earned income go unreported might seem way more serious than an eighth grade mistake, the belief that consequences accompany choices must start somewhere. For me, I feel fortunate that I learned this lesson in music class and not in a jail cell.

But this example seems too obvious because everyone knows cheating is wrong, right? Apparently not.

A Rutgers University study shows that 75 percent of 4,500 high school students surveyed cheat.[8] One student commented, "I actually think cheating is good. A person who has an entirely honest life can't succeed these days."

In other words, consequences for the choice to cheat either don't exist or stand as inconsequential. For a moment, substitute the picture I painted of cheating on a music test with a young child taking something that isn't his. Or hitting people. Or swearing, lying, or talking back to a parent. Or ignoring rules at school or church. If someone like Mrs. Mumaw isn't watching and ready to dish out appropriate measures, how will kids learn — and from whom?

The same Rutgers study asked students why they cheat. Other than academic pressure, the most common response was the adult world's poor example. "I think kids today are looking to adults and society for a moral compass," says Professor Donald McCabe, "and when they see the behavior occurring there, they don't understand why they should be held to a higher standard."[9]

It's up to *you* to teach your children this lesson, which will help them choose well all their days.

> The highway of the upright avoids evil; those who guard their
> ways preserve their lives.   *Proverbs 16:17*

Stop and Start

You will begin to teach that life has consequences when you stop covering for your child or intervening on his behalf. Let him go to school with no excuse note from you when he feels too tired to wake up on time or his homework remains undone because he played video games all evening. If you insist on clearing his path of any rocky situations lest he stumble, you will enable a consequence-free — and distorted—view of life. A belief will emerge that life will work out just fine no matter what he does or doesn't do.

A University of California, Irvine, study paints a shocking picture of what such a child looks like when he leaves home. Out of 466 students at a large public university, almost 41 percent believe that they deserve a B in any class for merely completing most of the assigned reading, and 34 percent feel they should receive a B for attending most of a course's classes.[10] Do you think these students learned as children that consequences exist if you fail to do your homework or don't show up when you're supposed to?

According to psychologists Tim Clinton and Gary Sibcy, parents who constantly cover for or overprotect children do so because they don't want their children to experience any suffering or pain.[11] Legitimate pain and normal suffering, however, serve as important building blocks toward maturity. According to Romans 5, "We know that suffering produces perseverance; perseverance character; and character, hope."

> I have told you these things, so that in me you may have peace. In this world you will have trouble. But take heart! I have overcome the world. (John 16:33)

"This means letting them face life experiences and people that will stretch them. And while they're learning and developing, dusting them off and getting them back in the race," says Clinton and Sibcy.[12]

Parents who allow children to face and feel consequences will help them understand the cause and effect produced by their decisions. For greatest impact, start now.

Ben began this lesson early with his children. "One day as we drove in the car, my five-year-old son started throwing candy at his sister," he says. "I told him that if he didn't stop right away, he would go to his room when we arrived at home and would receive discipline.

I watched him in the mirror. He looked at me, and then threw one more piece of candy. So I told him, 'That's it.'

"As we pulled in the driveway, I told him to go immediately to his room and I'd be up there soon. When I opened his door a few minutes later, he looked up at me and said, 'Daddy, can't we just pray about this instead?'

"We didn't pray."

Well done, Ben. His son tried to avoid facing and feeling the consequences of a bad choice. Instead, he learned the reality that consequences exist. Regardless of discipline style, parents who reliably back up words with actions teach their children well. A focus-group teenager affirmed the lasting impact consistency in this area brings: "My parents always had rules. I only ever broke each of them once, though, because my parents also always had a consequence to back up the rule — so I definitely learned."

It's never too late to start, although the stakes tend to rise from throwing candy to throwing away opportunity. A mom with a high school son shares what this lesson can look like with an older child.

"Our son is highly intelligent, but is also unorganized, a procrastinator, and doesn't seem to care," says Denise. "We give him coaching but let him make decisions on how to use time. He should be getting A's. Instead, due to his poor choices, he's getting B's and C's. He is going to learn that those choices will cost him opportunities for academic scholarships and, as a result, he'll have to carry more debt from student loans."

Denise and her husband know that to cover for their son today will hinder his maturity and ability to thrive in life later — even when he must continue learning difficult lessons as a high school student. When the report card arrives, or the first loan payment comes due, he'll hopefully understand how consequences work. He'll know that his choices matter. He'll feel legitimate, value-adding pain.

Fortunately, his mom and dad resist the urge to cover for his transgressions, even in his late teens, so that he'll learn a long-term, beneficial lesson. As Denise says, "Let them cry now or they'll make you cry later."

Applaud and Talk

Discussions about consequences often focus on bad choices and negative outcomes. Picture the superstore-like volume and variety of poor-decision options that tempt kids. Can parents allow a child to make enough mistakes to learn all he needs to know from bad consequences? Of course not.

Instead of constantly pointing out wrong choices, give generous attention to smart decisions. Consider the following perspective changes:

- As mentioned earlier, studies show that up to 75 percent of high school kids cheat.[13] That means 25 percent make a good moral choice and deserve encouragement.
- Thirty-seven percent of eighth graders report they've used alcohol.[14] That means 63 percent made better choices and could probably benefit from affirmation.
- A poll showed that elementary students spend, on average, seventy-eight minutes per night on homework.[15] Other research shows that eight- to ten-year-olds consume between seven and eight hours of media daily.[16] Occasional congratulations seem appropriate for a child willing to keep the screens turned off so that studies receive full attention and effort.

When a child receives positive remarks for making good choices, the likelihood increases that he or she will seek to make the right decision when facing other circumstances. The key to success is to catch your kid choosing well. But that's just the starting point.

To make the most out of these catches, intentionally talk about them and use the consequences as a discussion point. "Some kids were caught drinking. What do you think will happen to them? I'm really proud of you for saying no and not jeopardizing your future." Or, "You must feel great about making the smart choice to get your homework done before playing any video games. A lot of kids get that order wrong—what do you think happens to their grades?"

Parents fool themselves if they believe that kids who display good decision-making will continue to do so with no reinforcement.

Management and leadership guru Marcus Buckingham believes that employers who withhold praise for an employee's good behaviors will, over time, see less of these behaviors. "Having behaved in a certain way and been ignored for it, the employee will start to change his behavior in order to get some kind of reaction from you," Buckingham says.[17]

A strong parallel exists to parenting. Whether or not he realizes it, every person walks through life a decision away from unwanted consequences. The more you can encourage your child to step clear of bad decisions, by talking and applauding when he does well, the more you can expect the child to live into your affirmation.

And when your child makes mistakes, use dialogue in tandem with the consequence in order to avoid a repeat offense. A focus-group teenager explains what this looks like: "When my parents talk to me about my mistakes, they don't simply say, 'This is wrong, so don't do it,' and then punish me. Before I face the consequence, they ask me to explain why it was wrong and why I shouldn't do whatever I did."

Any parent can get angry and punish a child. Adept and intentional parenting always looks for the lesson—and that pays off.

"Their patience has helped me

> Finally, brothers and sisters, rejoice! Strive for full restoration, encourage one another, be of one mind, live in peace. And the God of love and peace will be with you.
>
> (2 Corinthians 13:11)

develop my own sense of right and wrong," the teen concludes. "So now, every problem I face isn't so hard for me to figure out the right thing to do."

Show and Tell

If, at this point in our lesson, you believe you need an approach that's even more powerful than encouragement and talking, you're absolutely right. As the late James Baldwin, author and social commentator, once wrote, "Children have never been very good at listening to their elders, but they have never failed to imitate them."[18]

Your challenge: Show your children that you too face consequences for your actions. Steve shares a practical example: "While driving on a recent trip to Florida, I became angry with my wife," he says. "The consequence? I felt deep regret because I ruined the trip for everyone. So I admitted this to my kids, said that I was wrong, and told them about my need to seek my wife's forgiveness."

Another couple, Jarrett and his wife, Nancy, agree and offer counsel on the important next step. "We've modeled for our kids the idea that you not only have to apologize, but you also have to go back to people and fix whatever wrong you did," he says.

Jack describes how this wisdom worked for him. As a youth, he broke into a neighborhood store at night and stole several items. The police never solved the crime. Three decades later, he felt personally convicted about his actions. So he traveled several hours, returned to the store, admitted to the owner what happened, and paid (with exorbitant interest) for the damage and items he took. Most relevant to this chapter, he shared with his family about the shame he felt for years and the steps he took to right a wrong. Imagine the lesson his kids learned as they watched their dad make this confession.

While we can certainly learn plenty from our mistakes, most people would prefer to learn from *someone else's* mistakes. As appropriateness dictates, tell your children about the consequences you've faced. When you do, you'll give them a point of reference to remember when they face similar choices.

Wisdom tells us that life features an unending supply of consequences—so the faster your child learns this truth, the better. "If something bad happens, think of it this way," says a focus-group student. "Even though you're in trouble now, sometime in your life it's probably going to happen again. And that next time, if you decide to make a good decision, you won't have to face a consequence that's even worse."

> Be very careful, then, how you live—not as unwise but as wise.
>
> *Ephesians 5:15*

QUESTIONS FOR REFLECTION OR DISCUSSION

1. What does your child fear? Do you reinforce that fear or dispel it?
2. Describe the consequences your child has felt for a bad decision. Did he learn from that experience or did he become a repeat offender?
3. Which lesson does your child need to learn the most, to forget unimportant stuff or to remember life has consequences? Why?

BE A PEOPLE PERSON / BE YOUR OWN PERSON

The fear of human opinion disables.
PROVERBS 29:25, *THE MESSAGE*

Be a People Person

Nobody chooses to be like Mike. One of several children, his single mom works hard to support her family. They can afford little and must squeeze into a home in the projects several rooms too small. When mom isn't at work, she's too tired to pay attention to her children. Out of necessity, they have all learned to fend for themselves at home, in school, and on the street. Mike, the youngest, has long kept to himself. His age plus his slighter-than-average size so often resulted in people picking on him that he began avoiding attention from anyone older. "Adults don't care about me, so I don't care about them" summed up his sentiments.

Then school began, and his worldview began to change.

A first-grade teacher saw Mike as a timid little boy with big potential. She believed he needed the very thing he avoided—a reliable adult in his life—so she arranged to match him with a mentor. Randall, a professional engineer, volunteered through his church to meet with Mike during school for one hour each week. In addition to filling a relational need in this youngster's life, Randall also taught

Mike basic interpersonal skills. Little did either of them know the day would soon come when those lessons would serve him well.

Every January, our country observes National Mentoring Month, a commemoration few people know about. Randall sure didn't. Imagine his surprise when he and Mike received an invitation to attend a White House celebration held to recognize mentors and mentees. Days later, after purchasing a nice set of clothes for Mike, Randall drove the two of them three hours to Washington, D.C. They made their way through security and eventually stood inside the East Room at 1600 Pennsylvania Avenue — filled with wonder at the sights inside of a place most recognized by its iconic exterior.

After listening to various notables share their remarks, Randall and Mike wove through the audience and wound up standing at the front of a line that President Barack Obama and his wife walked past as they left the room. Fortunately, a cute and determined first-grader can maneuver and cut better than many Washington, D.C., insiders. Unfortunately, in the densest area of a room crowded with eager adults, Mike blended in with the pants and coattails. All the faces, smiles, and comments took place two feet above his head.

Mike, however, remembered Randall's coaching. In the weeks leading up to the celebration, Randall had taught Mike how to make good eye contact and to properly shake someone's hand, and they had practiced it over and over. Just as Michelle Obama drew near, Mike smiled and stuck out his little hand — with his head pointed almost straight up in an attempt to make eye contact.

An unexpected and irresistible sight, no doubt.

By putting basic people skills to use, a young boy who more typically avoided adult interaction captured the attention of our nation's first lady — and dozens of cameras too. She bent down on one knee, grabbed his hand with both of hers, returned his eye contact and smiled, and talked with Mike for a moment.

For the rest of his life, Mike will believe in the value of interacting with others. And he'll likely remain grateful that a guy named Randall loved him enough to show him how to be a people person — and to be ready to meet anyone.

How would your child have reacted in the same situation?

Of course, few children will ever visit the White House. Fewer still will meet the important people who live there. Mike did have these remarkable opportunities, but had he shyly stood close to the safety of his mentor's side, he might have missed an incredible experience. Did he rise to the occasion on his own? Unlikely. Kids rarely learn new people skills in the midst of important moments. Instead, give credit to the practical, hands-on lessons Randall taught Mike for several months prior to their grand experience.

From a house in the projects to the White House and any setting between, an individual's ability to relate with others matters plenty. People skills enhance one's social life. Even young children can, with parental help, make and keep relationships. And as years go by, confidence in interacting with people grows even more important, whether in classroom participation, group projects, oral presentations, job interviews, or client meetings. Not to mention meeting that special someone and fully participating in church life. Can people truly love one another, as the Bible commands, if they struggle to interact with others?

Unfortunately, some parents prefer to protect their kids rather than encouraging them to engage people. Ultimately, according to veteran parent Kevin, shielding children becomes a bad choice: "If we had let our kids hide behind us in public and make excuses for them like 'She's just shy' when they were young, they would have developed some bad habits."

Fortunately, a better way exists, according to Kevin's wife, Lisa: "So we would tell our kids that if they didn't greet an adult, it was unacceptable behavior. But we didn't just chastise them; we helped them understand what they should have done."

Kevin and Lisa invested relatively brief periods of time directing role-playing situations at home, through which they mimicked reality and gave guidance. "I might ask, 'We go to the store, and there's Mrs. Evans. What will you do?'" says Lisa. "At first, Kevin would provide answers such as, 'I'm going to look her in the eye, shake hands with her, and say hello.' Eventually, we asked the kids to describe what *they* would do, to make sure they understood and remembered the specifics. After all, we won't always be there with them."

> The righteous are as bold as a lion. (Proverbs 28:1)

Following at-home instruction and role-playing, steer kids toward opportunities for practical experience. Encourage your children to initiate interaction at the store with your version of Mrs. Evans — and with the checkout people as well. Church presents a nonthreatening setting where you'll find many people willing to talk — so encourage children to speak with individuals of every age (especially the pastor, who often appears intimidating to kids). The same goes for the server at a restaurant, the teenage ticket taker at the theater, and the old guy who drives the bus.

To help my children learn people skills, I often take one of them with me when I travel for speaking engagements. They've learned to greet, laugh, and swap stories with folks from Traverse City, Michigan, to Fort Worth, Texas, to Mississauga, Ontario. I long for them to live into the words attributed to poet Adam Mickiewicz: "The nectar of life is sweet only when shared with others."[1]

If this lesson seems too inconsequential to merit your concern, consider the comments from a focus-group teen who admitted that she had to learn to share life the hard way. "My mom wasn't much of a people person when she was young," the student said. "Not to be mean, but she doesn't have a lot of friends now. So I learned to go out and make friends and be nice to people — or look what will happen."

Whether age four or fourteen, our kids deserve better than a learn-it-on-your-own approach, so let's help them become people persons by focusing on five parts of the body—arranged from the easiest to the most challenging.

Hands

A sixth-grade boy and his dad attended a youth-sport-league registration day with hundreds of other fathers and sons. Near the end of the day—after this father-son combo had stood in numerous lines for hours to complete paperwork, try on equipment, and (most importantly) pay exorbitant participation fees—the league commissioner pulled the dad aside. "Your son was the only boy all day who offered his hand and gave me a firm shake, looked me in the eye, and asked me how I was doing," he said. "How did you do it?"

The easy answer for this dad? "Practice."

I still remember how my own handshake evolved. Every Sunday at church, our pastor asked all in attendance to stand and greet one another. Our family routinely sat in front of the Nicholson family. Mr. Nicholson worked as our school principal, which is the reason why I still refer to him as "Mr." For years, Mr. Nicholson commented on the strength of my handshake. He possessed an unusually strong grip, and he kept hold of my hand until I returned significant force, sometimes for an uncomfortably long time.

Eventually, his encouragement turned into a personal mission—I wanted to break his hand! For a few moments before the meet-and-greet portion of the service, I'd stretch and flex my muscles to produce maximum power. More than four decades later, I often remember and appreciate him whenever I offer someone a firm shake. Funny, of all the coaching I received as a youngster, his stands out as some of the most valuable.

Seriously? A firm handshake matters enough to qualify as an important lesson kids need to learn? Yes, but only if your child expects to work one day. Picture your son or daughter years from now as you consider these words from a CNN online article:

> Prospective employers said they're more likely to overlook visible body piercings and tattoos than an ineffective handshake, according to a 2001 survey of human resources professionals. Plus, when you shake hands with people upon meeting, they're two times more likely to remember you than if you didn't shake hands, according to a study by the Incomm Center for Trade Show Research.[2]

Eyes

Ten-year-old Audrey enjoys bedtime because that's when she usually has Mom's or Dad's attention all to herself—no siblings to compete with for air time. Recently, after her dad tucked her in and turned the lights off, she began to tell him the story of what she experienced at school that day. A few minutes into her description, though, she noticed Dad multitasking.

He stood in her doorway with his ear pointing toward Audrey as he stared down the hallway. He had looked forward all day to time with his wife, and he wanted to make eye contact with her to cue their quickly approaching moments together. Audrey kept talking, her voice louder and louder as Dad kept looking at Mom. Finally, as if startled awake, he realized his daughter's volume had reached a shout level.

> You have stolen my heart with one glance of your eyes. (Song of Songs 4:9)

Unaware of the reason, he said, "Audrey, keep it down, please."

"Daddy, then show me your eyes when I'm talking to you," she demanded.

The eyes play an irreplaceable role in connecting with people. Studies have shown that babies as young as two days old can detect when someone looks directly at them.[3] Intuition prompts us to understand that the purpose of those dense, colorful spheres is much greater than simply the ability to see out into the world. Because the eyes serve as windows to the soul, children from a very early age are eager to peek inside.

Conversely, it comes as little surprise to experience awkwardness when you talk with a person who consistently looks away as you speak. However unintentional, avoiding eye contact sends a variety of nonverbal messages, including lack of interest, caring, confidence, or even integrity. The same signals are evident when someone looks away from you as *they* talk.

Eye contact is a must to become a people person. And once again, practice serves as the pathway to mastery. No, you need not engage your children in stare-downs to see who blinks first. Instead, put down the paper, look up from the computer, or turn away from the television when your child speaks to you. And don't sneak little peeks back throughout your conversation. At meals, look more at whom you are eating with than at what you eat. Whenever you prioritize your child by showing her your eyes, she knows she's valued. At the same time, you teach her the difference that her own eye contact makes to others.

Ears

I believe the people who say that listening is an act of love. The ability to hear and understand another person serves as a powerful people skill. But it too requires development.

My family routinely poses the question "What was your favorite part of the day?" to one another during meals. Here's the catch: in our family of four, this conversation requires each person to listen for three-fourths — and talk only one-fourth — of our time together. While we enjoy updates on math tests, tennis practice, and the great joke a friend told at lunch, we also learn.

We learn, for instance, how to listen without the need to speak right away. We discover how to wait for our turn to talk. To pay attention to what someone else believes is important. To not interrupt — in fact, we throw a verbal penalty flag on anyone who commits the interruption blunder. We put into practice the advice of Dr. Peter Newhouse, from the organization Winning At Home: "The word 'listen' contains the same letters as the word 'silent.' It's impossible to listen if you do all the talking."[4]

We don't answer the phone during meals either. The same goes for texting and television. "I suspect with all the cell phones and iPods that kids aren't showing respect to people as much anymore," says

Melissa, a veteran mom. "Instead, they ignore the people around them to listen to a song or watch a video."

To listen shows respect, and respect is a requirement for every people person.

Mouth

Becky and I look forward to a comment we consistently hear during our son's parent-teacher conferences. You see, Scott captures his teachers' attention each year with what he says. Specifically, he asks them, "How are you?" when he arrives in class, and then wishes them a good day before he leaves. Two simple statements for a total of seven words. Can it truly be that simple to make a strong and positive impression? Yes. And did he learn this impression-building skill from me? No.

While I tend to get impatient with my wife for her time-consuming greetings whenever we enter a room of people—and for her longer-than-I-want farewells when we leave—Becky models this skill very effectively for our children. She, and now they, effortlessly display people-person abilities I must work hard to achieve.

If teaching in this skill area rested solely on my shoulders, I'd run the risk of do-as-I-say-not-as-I-do disingenuous coaching. Karl, a focus-group parent, feels the same. "I have to watch and guard myself," he says, "so that I don't have a different standard of engaging people than I want my children to always have." Our kids deserve better.

Children also need someone to explain how and when to initiate greetings and well-wishes. And they need encouragement to always insert a person's name into the conversation. The responsibility rests on parents to show their child how to ask questions in an attempt to know more about a person, which communicates personal interest.

Another parent, Janice, concurs on the need to model well. "I would always tell my children stories about the interesting people I met at my job working in a retail store," she said. "Hearing me talk about those whom I had met helped my kids develop intrigue about people and the desire to find out about others."

Lindsey, another mom who wants her children to possess strong people skills, offered insight on an additional valuable aspect of learning in this area—that of correction.

"I called my daughter on her cell phone and she answered by saying 'What?' I told her, 'What? How about you give me back the phone you're talking on right now that's in my name. I'll give you just one more chance.' Then I hung up and called her back. She answered, 'Hi, Mom, how are you?'"

Feet

To give the previous four areas traction requires deliberate action. Said another way, to be a people person requires a person to walk out of his comfort zone. Consider the various motions we've already covered:

- *Step* toward another person and *extend* your hand to shake.
- *Move* your eyes away from anywhere else to *make and keep* eye contact with the other person.
- *Hold* back your own words to actively *listen* to the other person.
- *Offer* a greeting, *call* someone by name, and *ask* them a question to demonstrate your interest.

Just as a bike remains a useless object unless someone rides it, people skills possess no value unless they're put to use. So help your child onto the seat, then give a little push. Ask your son to answer the door when you expect guests and look for the reaction to his handshake. Encourage him to ask a store clerk a question and watch his eyes. Challenge your daughter to initiate conversation at dinner, especially when relatives sit around the table. Give your child an errand to run that requires her to walk to a neighbor's house and ring the door-bell. Countless opportunities exist to put learning into practice, as long as your child makes the move—which might also require some action from your own two feet. "I've discovered that, on occasion, my children interact with other adults much better if I walk away and they can't rely on me," says Marcia.

Perseverance Required

One spring, my then four-year-old-son, Scott, decided the time had come to take the training wheels off his bike. So when the snow completely cleared off the sidewalks, we began his learning process. "Always look at where you're going, and keep pedaling for balance," I said through labored breaths from jogging beside him with my hand on his seat back for balance.

On our second day, we noticed other kids playing outside. Scott particularly noticed Jenna, a cute girl two years his senior. My son decided to impress her with his fresh talent, so he asked me to let go and stop running three houses away from where Jenna stood. I honored his brave request and watched him pedal away on his own. Two houses later, the story changed.

Scott looked up to see if Jenna spotted him, which meant he momentarily took his eyes off the sidewalk. At the same instant, his front wheel hit a crack. Not the kind that might break your mother's back; those are common. The kind that waits like a land mine for an unsuspecting victim. This jagged fissure jolted his front wheel enough to turn the bike into the grass. To his credit, Scott kept pedaling. Even after he'd hit the single leftover snow pile. As I ran, feeling like I moved in slow motion, he kept pedaling. I watched my precious son's bike slow to a stall and then fall like a tree cut by a logger.

Before I reached him, he sprang up and with a forced smirk turned toward our house. When he felt confident Jenna could not see his face, I saw the agony of humiliation distort his smile. Inside our house, tears flowed. We talked about the need to bravely jump back on that bike and ride again. "Okay," he said, "but can we wait until Jenna goes inside?"

No matter what, kids need to learn to keep pedaling. Patiently allow your child to fully develop, over time, as a people person. Expect that along the way, you'll encounter successes and setbacks, smooth sidewalks and cracks.

> Give careful thought to the paths for your feet and be steadfast in all your ways. (Proverbs 4:26)

"Recently, a man at church tried to engage with my son and ask him questions about activities he knew my son enjoyed," Silas says. "Rather than join the conversation as we've discussed, my son simply provided one-word answers and a lot of 'uh-huh' responses. Back home that day, I talked with him about the importance of answering questions with full thoughts, and even to ask a question back.

"I called the man, a friend, and asked him if we could try again sometime. This man found us the next weekend and repeated the process. My son did a much better job and later admitted he felt a lot better about it."

A world that constantly shifts offers challenges too. "Society has changed," observes Stan. Fortunately, he offered yet another nugget of wisdom: "So we stress to our kids that they should show honor and respect, and greet people regardless of how well they're received."

Practice involves friends and peers in addition to adults. In fact, interaction with other children serves as a safe starting point for people-skill development. A teen explains how: "I've always been very shy, especially when I was younger," she says. "So my parents helped me, like times when they would say, 'Why don't you have her over?' and I'd say, 'I don't know her very well.' They'd always reply, 'That's how you get to know someone.'"

Unlike training wheels, the need for guidance in young children doesn't disappear; it changes as they grow. "My husband was very deliberate and specific with our son on how he should show honor and respect to girls," says Meredith. "One time after a dance, we found out he didn't do a good job with several common courtesies, and the girl left the dance with other people to take her home. The next day, my husband took my son and together they drove to the girl's house, and my son apologized to her dad for not being an honorable date and bringing his daughter back home."

I hope the parents of my kids' future spouses teach like Meredith and her husband do today. You likely want a people person for your kids too.

. . .

A people person who tries too hard, however, risks becoming a people pleaser. As Bill Cosby once said, "I don't know the key to success, but the key to failure is to try to please everyone." A girl with strong people skills who believes she must always cater to others to win them over places herself on a treadmill that never stops. Along the way, she runs a great risk of losing out on who God made her to be.

To develop as a people person, we looked at several body parts. To ensure a people person maintains healthy balance, though, requires the use of just one—the one we'll examine next in our counterpart lesson.

Be Your Own Person

God uniquely created every person. And within each of us he placed a brain that, among many other functions, houses our decision-making abilities. A key decision that children (and adults) constantly face is, "Will I do what I know is right?"

As a child and youth, I frequently heard a frustrated demand—often paired with an equally perplexing question: "David, use your brain!" Then, "David, what were you *thinking*?" Unfortunately, those words came after my mistakes and were lost in thick ambiguity, similar to my standard reply, "I don't know." It was an honest response, actually, as it indicated little or no forethought to whatever I had done. And it was prima facie evidence that guidance was necessary.

The lesson to be one's own person starts when parents accept the responsibility to shape a child's ability to learn wise decision-making skills—and to continue doing so from his earliest years through his late teens. Eventually that son will face situations without mom or dad nearby to help determine the path to take. To make good choices, he'll need judgment that's independent of friends, media, and other influences. Will you prepare him to be his own person?

The process starts when parents allow young children to make choices that require an opinion or, ideally, that point out trade-offs and potential sacrifices. Decisions about brushing teeth, finishing dinner, or hitting a sister don't qualify because only one option exists—obedience.

On the other hand, let a daughter make the choice of whether to join a tennis league or a dance troupe, whether or not to finish her homework now so she can watch *American Idol* later, or to decide between chicken nuggets and a cheeseburger. Parents who make every choice for a child stunt her decision-making skills development. "You choose" moments serve as opportunities for kids to grow and mature, even though they take more time, patience, and restraint. Oh, how tempting to jump in and shout, "She'll take the four-piece meal with honey mustard dipping sauce!"

Children flourish when they travel through life confident in themselves rather than constantly looking to others for decisions, identity, or solutions.

Eventually, the stakes fly much higher than chicken nuggets. Relatively low-impact choices one day become situations that call for good discernment the next. For that reason, to be his or her own person requires a child to have practiced boldly making the right decisions. Many varieties of "right" exist, so prepare to teach a multidimensional lesson.

Easy vs. Right

Decisions between the right thing to do and an easier alternative typically involve a choice between doing nothing (easy) and an option that carries a cost (right). Consider the following four common scenarios shared by parents, tales of teachable moments that involve the kind of costs we should encourage our kids to pay.

1. Sometimes the right thing costs money and initiative

"While many holidays involve a month or more of publicity and awareness, Mother's Day sneaks up on us every year. A few days, or sometimes a few hours, before the big day arrives, I remember that we need to do something for my wife. My kids would prefer that I handle buying a gift and card, so they could simply sign their names. Sure, it's easier for me to take care of everything than for them to use their own cash or put effort in and do the shopping, but that seems unwise."

2. Sometimes the right thing costs time and courage

"My first-grader brought home materials for his school's fundraiser. The school even assigned a minimum goal for each student; talk about pressure! I know the easiest way to take care of this is for me to call several neighbors and ask for their support. Should I make the calls or insist that he take an afternoon and walk to each house, ring the doorbell, and make his pitch?"

3. Sometimes the right thing costs effort and comfort

"As we came to a stop at an intersection, we noticed a strong wind gust blow an elderly man's hat off his head and down the sidewalk. With every step he shuffled, the hat danced a few more feet away. The blowing rain made us want to stay in the car and out of the storm. Take the easy road and drive away, or get out and get wet?"

4. Sometimes the right thing costs pride

"Our church used a camping theme to decorate the children's ministry area. When we arrived home late Sunday morning, my son had an extra stuffed animal that we realized came from church. He owns one bear, not two—we knew he had thought it was his bear, and we knew it had to go back. We had a choice: to return it next weekend as we passed by the décor or to drive back now to hand it back to the director and admit what happened."

As you read all four scenarios, the right choice seems clear. Had you participated personally in any of them, though, you might have felt each moment's tension—a squeeze that cuts off the flow of an adult's good judgment and makes the easy route look good.

The real question, though: How would a child respond?

Answer: In a manner that's consistent with his or her experience. What you've taught and modeled matters, of course. But so does what you've reinforced. To that end, constantly call out a child's great choices: "Way to go; you made the right decision." She'll need the confidence that your words build, because life acts like a drawbridge, increasing the gap between the easy and the right. Every person chooses which side to occupy, and that choice matters to more than just mom and dad.

"If you love me, you will obey what I command," Jesus said. Turn the other cheek, carry equipment an extra mile, love your enemies—none of his commands qualify as easy and many involve a price.

In their book *Do Hard Things*, teen authors Alex and Brett Harris share wisdom beyond their years when they advise, "When we make a decision to obey God — even when it costs us something — and to live out our faith in our day-to-day life, it will be hard, but it will be good."[5]

Popular vs. Right

Popularity exerts quite a pull. Why? Research shows popularity in school brings many advantages. One study concluded: "Compared with unpopular students, popular students are emulated and approached more often by others, receive more help, are the recipients of more positive stereotypes, and maintain more positive relationships with others."[6]

Not a bad list.

Problems arise, however, from the *quest* for popularity. For many children, the path to the promised land of being well known and admired requires the traveler to first achieve peer acceptance. The desire for others to welcome you, like you, or think well of you can lead to allowing others to make decisions for you.

That's a serious problem. Mom or Dad, time to step in and teach — or watch your child morph into a person you no longer know.

> Dear children, do not let anyone lead you astray.
> (1 John 3:7)

One teen offered a typical scene from a school lunchroom, and an example of a mom who dishes up nutritious advice: "Meredith always tries to make our whole lunch table wear the same thing," said the student. "But my mom says that if I don't want to wear what Meredith says, then I really don't have to. She's right; Meredith can't make a person out of me!"

Parental discernment serves as a necessary ingredient. A table of girls deciding that Friday is green day poses no threat to a daughter's well-being. When she begins to feel pressure to acquiesce to someone else's demand—and here's the key—*when she doesn't want to*, then a parent needs to help navigate. Little issues like wardrobe selections eventually mature into weightier issues. So the same must be true of your judgment. In addition, keep your eyes open for times when children put your advice to work so you can affirm their decisions to opt for what's right rather than for what's popular.

Initially, those victories might prove difficult to recognize.

"Our kids stayed home most Saturday nights, and at first that bothered us," says Chris. "Then we figured out that they didn't want to do the stuff other kids were doing. If we had forced them too much to be people persons who fit in more, they might have gotten in trouble."

Wrong vs. Right

I once worked in a church that featured two large video screens in its auditorium. Occasionally, pastors would refer to them as a tool for attendees to use when faced with right-versus-wrong decisions, saying, "If you wouldn't want all of us to watch what you're planning to do on these screens, then don't do it." That seemed like straightforward advice. Until a dad told me that he brought his five-year-old son into the auditorium, shared the exact same words, and regrets his attempt to use adult logic with a preschooler. "Now," the dad explained, "he won't take a bath."

Keep the issue of right and wrong simple. Repeat the messages "If it's wrong, don't do it" and "Don't hang around anyone who is doing something wrong." Talk about situations and ask your child to name the right thing to do. He or she will often know. When a teacher, coach, or any other leader provides your child with rules, spend a few moments reviewing them with your youngster—your attention will strengthen the rules and communicate their importance. Discuss when to tell a teacher or other authority about a wrong that took place—and, also, when to let it go.

Yes, there are times when it's better to keep quiet and move on.

My son relentlessly adheres to rules. This required me, I kid you not, to convince him at age six to stop turning himself in to the referees when he committed a foul in basketball that escaped their notice. Same thing for the need to apologize when whistled for an infraction.

On the other hand, you and I both know children who would benefit from a few more referees and a few more quick whistles.

Let's take right and wrong one step further. A child on a journey to be his own person will, at some point, find himself tangled up in situations that require him to take a stand for what he believes is right. Of course we want our children to adeptly handle such situations.

But Jackie's son Morris did not. He disagreed with a teacher about whether or not he completed an assignment on time. The argument moved quickly from personal conversation at his desk to loud public insults for the entire class to witness. Minutes later, Morris found himself in the principal's office, waiting for his parents, ejected from school for the day.

Jackie and her husband helped their son understand the lack of respect he had shown. At the same time, they also discussed appropriate ways to disagree. They even role-played with Morris. That evening, they called the teacher and asked for a meeting the next day. When all four sat together, Jackie and her husband said little. Instead, they let Morris and the teacher discuss how he could have respectfully handled the situation.

> My dear brothers and sisters, take note of this: Everyone should be quick to listen, slow to speak and slow to become angry, because human anger does not produce the righteousness that God desires. (James 1:19–20)

In the end, everyone agreed that it's okay to disagree and that there are right and wrong ways to handle a disagreement when both individuals think they are right. Other times, right and wrong—as well as the appropriate response—appear as easy to see as a squad car's lights in the night. "To help them be their own persons," says Karl, "we're coaching our teenagers to just leave a situation when others are doing stuff that's wrong." Another dad says, "We've told our kids over and over that you get in trouble when you hang out with trouble."

Directing kids to hit the exit was the advice most often mentioned by parents in every focus group, regardless of location. Keep in mind the level of parental involvement required before your son or daughter drives. "Calling us to come get them can be very awkward. So to make it easier for them, we have a code," says Linda. "They call and mention a predetermined statement, such as 'I think I left the oven on.'

"Of course I felt bad about the time when my son called, repeated our coded message, and I argued with him that there was no way he left the oven on. I even went to the kitchen and checked. I sure felt stupid later."

The time spent talking about how to make the right decisions in the face of inappropriate behavior will teach your child plenty about how to become his own person. Just be sure to remember the code.

Right Boundaries

The need for personal boundaries—physical and emotional lines no one can cross—also deserves mention. The specific lesson to consider concentrates on how to help your child insist that others honor his or her boundaries.

Seth learned an easy-to-overlook starting point to this lesson the hard way. "I hug a lot," he says. "But the day came when my daughter didn't want to hug. Instead, she gave me a side, half-hug. I insisted, though, and grabbed her and gave her a big hug. After she left the room, my wife told me to really think about my approach."

"You are the biggest, strongest boy she knows," said Seth's wife. "She needs to learn that her no means no with any boy. You can show her that no matter what, her no is final. But if you insist on getting what you want, you undermine that lesson." Wise observation.

Discuss boundaries with your child. Then honor those boundaries so he or she can see that they work. Your consistency will galvanize your child's belief that a line drawn can and should work.

That is, as long as lines—boundaries or other right decisions—never become walls. The possibility exists to take the "be your own person" lesson too far and live in isolation. In the book of Genesis, the Bible says that God looked at Adam and said, "It is not good for man to be alone." From the beginning, our Creator designed us to engage life with others, as individuals in relationship with other individuals.

- Be your own person.
- Be a people person.
- And above all, be God's person.

> For we are God's handiwork, created in Christ Jesus to do
> good works, which God prepared in advance for us to do.
> *Ephesians 2:10*

QUESTIONS FOR REFLECTION OR DISCUSSION

1. Which body part lesson (hand, eyes, ears, mouth, or feet) does your child need most?
2. Which lesson do you need the most?
3. On a scale of 1 (never) to 10 (always), rate your child's ability to make the right decisions when alone _____, with friends _____, or in your presence _____. How will you help her in each of these situations?

Find Your Unique Fit /
Find Out You Can Fail

Always be a first-rate version of yourself, instead
of a second-rate version of somebody else.
Judy Garland[1]

Find Your Unique Fit

Early in my career, I worked for a large corporation that provided an all-expenses-paid vacation for approximately 250 employees and their spouses. The opening night banquet featured, among many activities, a team karaoke competition. The first two teams showcased impressive talent.

Then it was our turn.

My team huddled together to select a song and the talent bold enough to sing. We landed on "Midnight Train to Georgia" by Gladys Knight and the Pips. "I loved that song when I was young," I whispered to my friend Gary, "and I still sing it when I drive."

I'm unclear about what happened next. My memory resumes with the bright lights, loud music, and three colleagues behind me trying to dance like the Pips. I still remember my voice over the PA system; hitting all the words on cue and trying to mimic the notes Gladys was singing in my mind. Although I thought the two voices were in sync, three signs indicated others might not fully agree.

First, people laughed. Even though the music's volume overpowered their chuckles, I could see them nearly doubling over. Could my Pips really be dancing so badly that people would react with such cruelty? Second, my wife appeared to be in pain. She exhibited a very similar expression, actually, to the one she wore moments before delivering our children. And finally, I noticed she was missing two items—a nametag and (although she debates this one) her wedding ring. As she met others during the rest of the evening, she used her maiden name.

Years later, now that we can calmly talk about the incident, Becky and I agree that three things created problems that evening. Major problems.

1. I'm not a talented African-American female singer.
2. I'm not a talented white male singer, either.
3. Because I thought I was both 1 and 2, I looked like an idiot and almost lost my job.

Together, those mistakes taught me a powerful lesson—one that continues to provide me with practical guidance. For instance, when my daughter brought home a note from her dance teacher asking for volunteers to perform in the Daddy Dance for her upcoming recital, my wife firmly said, "Gladys can't dance, either." My wife can keep her ring on; I know my fit in this world—and I am not meant to perform on stage.

So what's the big challenge?

Everyone possesses different talents and passions—as well as their own unique identity. And the child who discovers his or her personal fit will flourish. Many messages, though, contradict this reality and thrust kids toward conformity to an expectation or norm established by someone else.

Do this. Be like that. Here's the right way.

Consider how standardized achievement testing in school provides a limited definition of what's needed to succeed, or to achieve "honors" designation. Or how the role-model advertising, like the "Be like Lil' Wayne" iPhone app, urges young people to look more like a star than the person they see in the mirror. Parents pile on when they blurt out the question, "Why can't you be like _____?" (fill in the blank with the name of a sibling, cousin, peer — or "me"). Even the subtle message perpetuated at church that "to worship is to sing" may alienate those without the ability to carry a tune. Trust me.

While none of these seem all that negative or hurtful, they serve as examples of how children constantly receive guidance about whom they should be — sometimes as attractive suggestions, other times as firm edicts. As a result, children all too often stretch or squeeze into expectations placed on them, rather than enthusiastically discovering the comfortable fit their uniqueness creates.

Here's the truth: a poor test-taker who looks nothing like Lil' Wayne, who possesses different talents than his brother, and who has a voice as unpleasant as a midnight train's whistle can thrive in life. But only once I discover my unique fit. I am not a good Gladys, but I am a decent someone else.

Parents face two choices: They can either encourage or discourage a kid when it comes to trying new experiences, to discovering what he loves and what he doesn't, and to embracing or ignoring his this-is-definitely-you identity. Choose encouragement. Along the way your child will be more likely to appreciate variety and diversity in others,

> For you created my inmost being; you knit me together in my mother's womb. I praise you because I am fearfully and wonderfully made; your works are wonderful, I know that full well. (Psalm 139:13 – 14)

and will find the world offers unique opportunities for the one-of-a-kind person God created him or her to be.

Here's the challenge: Find that person—the "fearfully and wonderfully made" vibrant person knit together by God himself, according to Psalm 139. That person exists within every child.

. . .

This past Easter I typed a quick text greeting to everyone on my cell phone's contact list. Unfortunately, I failed to put my name in the message. So one person sent a quick reply: "who R U?"

That's *the* question. *Who R U?*

All children ask that about themselves as they journey through life. Three key messages, path markers to point the way, will encourage them to discover the answer.

1. B U Not Me

I look back over my son's life and see different eras defined by his personal interests. Fire trucks. Giant Legos. Star Wars. Little League baseball. Youth basketball. High school football. From the moment Scott decided which toys to put in his mouth and which ones would sit slobber-free in his playpen, he's made his way from one absorbing passion to the next. My role? Imitate fire-truck sirens, sit on the floor to construct a Lego city (and watch him knock it down), swing a light-saber like a Jedi, play catch in the street, shoot baskets in the driveway, and run pass patterns on the practice field. He calls the plays.

Some are fun. Many require a time sacrifice. All have been acts of encouragement for his interests, regardless of their alignment with my own. No clever words or wisdom required. Just jump in and go with the current. The river of joy flows fastest and deepest in a child when a parent joins him as he chases dreams. Whatever those dreams are at the moment.

Start with the belief that your child will like some, but not all, activities. Easy so far. Then take a critical step deeper, by accepting that your child will show aptitude in some, but not all, areas. Regardless of the proficiencies and prowess you possess, your child will own a set of competencies unique to him. It might be a larger set than yours; it might be smaller. Very likely it will be altogether different.

Several years spent coaching youth sports of all sorts taught me that the least talented child was typically not the most miserable player on the team; that designation belonged to the youngster whose skills or enthusiasm fell short of those of his parents. The river of joy dries up when a parent attempts to direct the current, or when a child is unduly influenced to chase a parent's dream.

Karl, a dad with two boys, understands this concept well. "I desperately want my sons to do what they want to do," he says, "and not what they think I want them to do." This is another easy aspiration to agree with, especially before a child actually displays his talent.

In the movie *The Red Violin*, a child prodigy plays the violin so well that his foster dad can only hear the opportunity to earn a fortune. The man applies intense pressure, despite the lad's heart ailment, to make the boy excel as he prepares for a performance in front of royalty. When the big day arrives, young Kaspar begins to play — but his heart gives out at that very same moment.

Yes, this movie portrays an extreme example of pushing a child too hard. Yet notice how many children lose heart for an activity because exceptional performance becomes the expectation they must deliver. Whether with a violin, a baseball bat, or a science book, a child must hold the dream. The journey must remain his.

And you, as the parent, need to roll with the changes.

Marge remembers one such change the year her son Jay played football — well, "played" in a manner of speaking, as he actually sat on the bench. During games in which Jay's team amassed sizeable leads, her son remained on the sidelines. "My son's greatest contribution to the team that year was as an encourager on the sidelines. Today, I'm proud of him because he has grown up to be a very good encourager to all sorts of people."

The world desperately needs encouragers like Jay.

2. U R U, Not Him or Her

In her book *Ten Things I Wish I'd Known—Before I Went Out into the Real World*, Maria Shriver shares a recipe for feeling bad about herself: "I carefully choose as a basis for comparison someone who has a stellar career. Then I ignore any other problems she has, any sacrifices she's chosen to make. Next, I discount any of my own assets—the talents, gifts, and abilities God gave me. Finally, I ratchet up my expectations for myself to way, way past what I'm capable of. And voila! I feel like dirt."[2]

Let's help our children avoid the bitter taste that comes from constant comparisons with others. All kids have their own, unique flavor.

The most likely place for a child to assess how she measures up to others? Home. This is especially true for younger brothers and sisters.

> We have different gifts, according to the grace given to each of us. (Romans 12:6)

While the concept of sibling rivalry carries instant name recognition, another insidious dynamic of the dysfunctional family is sibling mimicry. In this case, a child does not compete with a brother or sister; actually, the opposite occurs. Instead the need exists to be just like him or her, hiding the unique individual—until that person is exposed by façade fatigue.

Leslie saw how deep sibling mimicry can embed itself in a family with four children. "Our oldest son played soccer, our oldest daughter played soccer, and our youngest daughter played soccer," she says.

"After our youngest son went out for soccer, he announced he hated it. Everyone gasped!"

To teach her family about the value of uniqueness, this proactive mom decided to take action. "We had many family discussions that reminded him—and everyone—that it's okay for him—or them—to pursue other activities. Getting the siblings on board with that belief was important."

Proactive parenting to combat the urge to copy starts with keen awareness. Jon provides another valuable perspective: "I can quickly teach an unwanted lesson with too much praise for one of my sons. Because the other son will want to do the same thing to earn dad's praise."

While many parental moves escape notice (or so we believe), this one stands out in a valuable way: "My parents never compare me to my brother, and that makes me feel like they notice me," a focus-group teen says. "Even when I don't do as well on something as he does, they never compare the two of us in any way."

Focus-group dad Stephen cautions us, though, to avoid limiting this discussion to families with multiple children: "Our daughter is an only child, so she has no siblings to compare herself with. Instead, she measures herself against her friends. So she's not immune from the desire to compete with or copy other kids."

Reality check: you and your kids will talk about other children. And adults. So take the lead and discuss others without injecting or implying any reference to your children or yourself. When you celebrate the passions, talents, or accomplishments of a friend, neighbor, or schoolmate without making comparisons, you send the message, "She has a unique identity, so it's okay for you to have one too."

"We tried to always tell our kids—convince them—that they had something to contribute to the world, and so did everyone else," said Janice, a mother of three. "We wanted them to see that in others."

3. I Love the Real U

While discussing movies with me, a second-grader informed me that he owned several DVDs, including *Jaws*. "That movie makes me afraid to swim," I said.

"Dude, don't worry," my eight-year-old counselor said. "That shark wasn't real. It was a fake, so you're safe to get back in the water."

We live in an era where the difference between fake and real blurs. Especially on the Internet, which allows anyone to dive in and become whomever they wish. Why would a kid want to be someone else? According to researchers at Indiana University, the most frequent reasons children age nine to eighteen gave for engaging in identity changes were "social compensation (e.g., to feel less shy), social facilitation (e.g., to make friends) and self-exploration (e.g., to explore how others react to me)."[3]

Life today offers opportunities for kids who are dissatisfied with themselves to take on a whole new identity. What happens, though, if the contrived identity emerges as a more appealing alternative? Dangerous waters, indeed, because that child will stop searching for his or her unique fit.

"Who R U?" should not be a question with multiple correct answers. So use your front-row seat in a child's life to cheer and offer assurance that the real U is the best U. This happens when you observe a child's uniqueness and frequently use the words "I love you just as you are" (see chapter 1 lesson "Believe That You Matter").

A mentor working through our KIDS HOPE USA program described his young charge this way: "He has enough energy in him to light a small city. Unfortunately, he's received little guidance on behavior, so he frequently finds himself in trouble. He told me that his mom grew sick of him last year, decided she couldn't change him, and sent him to live with his dad—who seems quite uninterested in raising a son.

"I recently had a conversation with the dad, and he told me that he hoped I could do something to change his son and settle him down. The little guy stood next to us and heard every word.

"It's a tragedy. This young boy is funny, has a great imagination, and responds well to clear direction. He's a great kid who just needs boundaries. I wish his parents would see that and love him for who he is."

Your child needs someone to love him for the real person he is, whether energetic or reserved, a standout athlete or a sideline encourager, a violin virtuoso or a scary movie lover. Your encouragement toward his uniqueness will provide him with an indispensable character trait, described by poet E. E. Cummings, "It takes courage to grow up and become who you really are."[4]

• • •

An inconsistent relationship exists between a person's unique fit and his success. Some children display unusual giftedness or talent that results in accomplishments immediately apparent to all. Others require more time.

In fact, high grades, athletic prowess, or artistic acclaim might not provide the most reliable readings. According to Stanford psychology professor and researcher Dr. Carol S. Dweck, "More than three decades of research shows that a focus on effort—not on intelligence or ability—is key to success in school and in life."[5]

Had accomplishment served as the only criteria for determining a person's fit, the coach who cut Michael Jordan from his high school freshman basketball team would have ended this basketball legend's career. An important lesson must accompany a child's quest for his unique fit in life, one that unleashes a willingness to put forth effort when the outcome remains uncertain.

Because uncertainty in life is a sure thing.

Find Out You Can Fail

Everyone fails. Yet life goes on.

Too many children, equipped and expected to go far, possess little ability to handle falling short. Children unable to deal with defeat create misery—for themselves and for those around them.

Conversely, the awareness to learn from a loss or the ability to show poise in disappointment reveals character richness. Parents serve kids well when they teach, model, and consistently reinforce how to appropriately accept failures and to move on. Along the way, children develop an ability to show grace to others who make mistakes—an excellent life skill, but one as uncommon as drivers who actually abide by the speed limit.

Rather than convincing kids to expect a smooth ride or a perpetual uphill climb, take a different route. You can send four key messages that will help children learn they can experience failure without *being* a failure. In fact, quite the opposite can prove to be true.

Fear Not (at Times You Will Fail)

"Fear of failure among children in America today is at epidemic proportions," says psychologist Dr. Jim Taylor. "Fear of failure causes children to experience debilitating anxiety before they take a test, compete in a sport, or perform in a recital. It causes them to give less than their best effort, not take risks, and, ultimately, never achieve complete success."[6]

A child who fears failure will avoid failure—and thereby avoid challenges. A child who avoids challenges misses opportunities to grow. As Robert Kennedy said, "Only those who dare to fail greatly can ever achieve greatly."[7]

Does your child avoid failure? Taylor suggests three ways that we parents can tell if that is the case. The first way is when a child avoids an activity—sometimes overtly, through refusal; other times more covertly through illness, injury, or forgetting/losing materials.

Second, the child might offer excuses, as in "That class is boring so I didn't care" or "The judges were unfair." When failure is not their fault, children can't be held responsible. And the third way is that the child will accomplish enough to avoid failure, but not enough to achieve full potential. Some students learn how to give enough effort to earn a B+ but remain afraid of the full commitment needed for A work.[8]

"Every teacher can tell the story of a student who needed to fail in order to be reassured that the world wouldn't come to an end," reports Nancy Gibbs in a *Time* magazine cover article on overparenting.[9]

So where does this fear of failure originate? Likely from you—the fact is that many parents are not okay with failing children.

If students need to learn they can live through failure, every mom and dad needs to learn the same lesson. Why? Because if we constantly shield a child from experiencing mistakes and disappointments, imagine the attitude they will automatically develop toward failure. While this seems like common sense, it's rarely practiced. "Nobody told us that, as parents, we shouldn't try to save our children all the time," a mother named JoAnne says.

True, the adrenaline rush feels good when we are a hero for our child. But over time, appreciation drops, replaced by expectation. And parents reach that point faster than a speeding bullet, as illustrated by a cartoon from Willis, a mere first-grader.

Linda, a parent of twin boys, admits to mixed feelings on this issue. "I don't want to be the parent who's always driving to school to take our kids what they left at home," she says. "But I also want to model grace and let them believe that they can count on me."

Many parents, though, have no hesitation about covering for their child, because inconvenience feels better than fear. The Gibbs' *Time* article put this issue under a microscope and delivered a bold diagnosis:

Fear is a kind of parenting fungus: invisible, insidious, perfectly designed to decompose your peace of mind. Fear of physical danger is at least subject to rational argument; fear of failure is harder to hose down. What could be more natural than worrying that your child might be trampled by the great, scary, globally competitive world into which she will one day be launched? It is this fear that inspires parents to demand homework in preschool, produce the snazzy bilingual campaign video for the third-grader's race for class rep, continue to provide the morning wake-up call long after he's headed off to college.[10]

Your child will fear failure as much or as little as you fear her failure. So leave the homework at home and keep the cape in the closet. Your child will survive and likely remember her homework more often on her own.

Try Hard (Even Though You Might Fail)

"When I play tennis, my parents always remind me that it is alright to lose if I tried my hardest and gave all I could give on the court," a teenager says. "It isn't about winning and losing in our house. Playing our best is what counts. And when we do lose, my parents aren't upset with me; they are proud that I tried and gave it all I could give."

Parents set the dial for the perceived acceptability level for failure. One setting reads "perfection only;" the other says "best effort." While the professional tennis circuit showcases high-achieving players who strive for perfection in their skills, the general population is filled with millions more who learned they couldn't live up to expectations. So they stopped trying to succeed—in anything. Where's your dial set?

Hint from experience: for maximum impact, share the "your best effort" perspective prior to challenges; that way you'll avoid sounding like you're awarding a consolation prize once the results are known. Repeat this message consistently, year after year, and a child will adopt this belief too. To start, though, many parents need an outlook change on success.

Here's one I recently came across. In her book *Mindset*, Dr. Dweck shares the reason for redefining success: "Yes, children love praise. And they especially love to be praised for their intelligence and talent. It really does give them a boost, a special glow—but only for a moment. The minute they hit a snag, their confidence goes out the window and their motivation hits rock bottom. If success means they're smart, then failure means they're dumb."[11]

So instead, affirm effort. Stubbornly.

As I worked on this chapter, my daughter, Erin, told me about the anxiety she felt about an upcoming geometry test. To this point, she has found schoolwork easy, and she has required relatively little effort to attain high grades. Now that geometry class was proving to be hard, she was starting to shut down. Rather than quiz her on the Pythagorean theorem (which I don't understand anymore—and neither do you), I challenged her effort level. "Give your best effort to preparing, more than you've done in the past, and you'll feel great about the test no matter what grade you get," I told her.

> Endure hardship as discipline. . . . No discipline seems pleasant at the time, but painful. Later on, however, it produces a harvest of righteousness and peace for those who have been trained by it. (Hebrews 12:7, 11)

I sure hope Dr. Dweck knows her stuff, I thought.

Oh, how tempting it felt to congratulate my daughter on the test grade she earned. I resisted, though, and instead congratulated Erin's pretest studies—and told her that the amount of work she applied is what she'll need to put in for the rest of her school years and in life overall. She agreed that the grade mattered less than the effort.

Weeks later, she did not fare as well on the final exam. Her (and my) focus on effort, however, remained intact. Through grades good and not-as-good, it is how hard you work that counts. You can look in a textbook to understand the Pythagorean theorem; you must look inside yourself to find the willingness to try hard.

In a speech to young people before he became president, then-Senator Barack Obama said, "Making your mark on the world is hard. If it were easy, everybody would do it. But it's not. It takes patience, it takes commitment, and it comes with plenty of failure along the way. The real test is not whether you avoid this failure, because you won't. It's whether you let it harden or shame you into inaction, or whether you learn from it; whether you choose to persevere."[12]

Learn Well (When You Do Fail)

While no one typically seeks failure, failure can indeed deliver positive aspects. Undesired experiences actually teach us to be more resilient, a lesson articulated in recent medical research: "Contrary to assumptions related to earlier studies, our research suggests that ultra-clean, ultra-hygienic environments early in life may contribute to higher levels of inflammation as an adult, which in turn increases risks for a wide range of diseases," said Thomas McDade, associate professor of anthropology at Northwestern University.[13]

Just as the body's immune system learns how to handle microbes of all sorts through experience, kids also learn to handle disappointment and keep going through experience. As author Randy Pausch described the process, "Experience is what you get when you didn't get what you wanted."[14]

For a lesson to take place following an undesired experience, mom and dad must remain awake at the wheel. Marianne's son is a very gifted student, but he has a problem with procrastination. One time, he waited until the night before the due date to work on a poetry notebook that should have required steady work for weeks. She says,

"After he turned it in, his teacher called me. I assured her that it was going to be a good lesson for him to receive an F. She was hesitant to give him the grade he deserved, but I insisted.

"He failed the assignment, but received the opportunity to rework the notebook and turn it in the next week for a maximum C grade. That was a very valuable lesson for him to learn—and one we didn't have to teach him or say 'I told you so' about."

Scott, a father with four kids at home, provides practical counsel to parents specifically concerned about school success and college admissions standards. "It's best to let your kids experience failure when they're young and grades don't really count," he says.

No matter the age, the realization that love and acceptance don't hinge on constant overachieving frees a child to relax and enjoy life. One focus-group student, who spent years stressed by an expectation that didn't exist, welcomed such freedom: "In fourth, fifth, and sixth-grade, I was getting upset because I wasn't getting A's on everything," this teenager says. "My parents said that it was okay to get a B, and that relieved the pressure I had put on myself."

Keep Going (Don't Let Failure Stop You)

Patty read a fascinating bit of wisdom on Facebook from her daughter's friend, likely an adapted quote commonly attributed to John Lennon: "If everything isn't okay in the end, maybe it's not the end."

Fortunately for many people, failure acts as a speed bump on the highway of success, not as an exit ramp. Consider how these folks kept going after an apparent failure.

- Decca Recording turned down four musicians following their first audition, believing that groups of guitars were on their way out of popularity. Ringo, George, John, and Paul kept going as the Beatles.

- Alexander Graham Bell demonstrated his new invention, the telephone, to President Rutherford B. Hayes. "That's an amazing invention, but who would ever want to use one of them?" was the response Bell heard. He kept going.
- The Grand Ole Opry fired a new singer after just one performance, telling him to get back to truck driving. That singer kept going; his name was Elvis Presley.
- Thomas Edison estimated that his experiments failed two thousand times before the light bulb worked. He kept going and is said to have remarked, "I never failed once. It just happened to be a 2,000-step process."

The likelihood is slim that your child or mine will end up a music legend or culture-changing inventor. However, less spectacular and more numerous possibilities exist for our kids to fully embrace life and contribute to it if they learn to keep going.

Sometimes, life hugs back.

Scott and I made a decent father-son team as we built his grand prix race car from a small wooden block. Our hopes accelerated every night we worked on his racer, as did our pulses when he placed it on the track for the first race one Saturday morning.

> They will have no fear of bad news; their hearts are steadfast, trusting in the LORD. Their hearts are secure, they will have no fear; in the end they will look in triumph on their foes. (Psalm 112:7–8)

As we both expected, our careful attention to critical details during the assembly quickly paid off as his car bolted to an early lead. With every foot traveled, we seemed to gain a larger advantage.

Then the unthinkable happened. His car lurched off the track and landed on the floor. He picked it up, and we stood together, silent, trying to piece together what had happened. I knew that when hope crashes, and it had, disappointment arrives soon afterward, followed by resentment and bitterness. Possibly even ugly emotions and outbursts. And, of course, regret.

I worried about how this might affect *him* too.

Fortunately, I had just enough common sense to offer these words: "Buddy, what a disappointment. I'm not sure how this happened, but let's not be bad losers. Even though we're out for the day, let's stay and cheer for other people to show we're good sports."

He agreed and we stayed. What a great choice.

In the next race, the same calamity struck another car. Ironically, race three featured a similar tragedy. Same in four. After the fifth straight crash, the race officials suspended action. Over an hour after the first wreck of the day, ours, they announced that lane six appeared to have a defect. All cars that crashed were invited back into the race.

We felt good that we had stuck around and resisted the urge to let failure derail us. We experienced unimaginable joy when Scott's car won the final race of the day!

Sure, we soaked up the thrill of winning a trophy for the fastest car. The road traveled that day, though, was a journey he and I will never forget. Help your child maintain a good attitude, even if he believes he's in a ditch. How? Keep going. Somehow, always keep going.

> Consider it pure joy, my brothers and sisters, whenever you
> face trials of many kinds, because you know that the testing
> of your faith produces perseverance. Let perseverance finish
> its work so that you may be mature and complete, not lacking
> anything.   *James 1:2–4*

QUESTIONS FOR REFLECTION OR DISCUSSION

1. What makes your child unique? Make a list of specific qualities, talents, and character traits. You can only affirm what you recognize and can name.

2. Consider the extent to which your child understands his uniqueness. Does he seem comfortable with himself, or does he try to act like someone else?

3. What is your attitude as you consider allowing your child to experience failure? What must change in you to maintain a healthy, long-term perspective toward failure?

Always Speak Up /
Only Speak the Truth

*Be who you are and say what you feel, because those who
mind don't matter and those who matter don't mind.*
Dr. Seuss

Always Speak Up

The day I learned the need to speak up remains a vivid childhood memory.

For some reason irrelevant to the story, my dad had sent me to my room. Typical of a five-year-old, this punishment seemed harsh for a moment, but only until I found something to occupy my solitary confinement. The new activity involved water, although I no longer recall the source. But whether it arrived via a cup, my goldfish bowl, or some other vessel, it landed on my pillow.

The responsible next step, I reasoned, was to get that pillow dry. No sense involving Dad any more than necessary. Besides, I had a plan.

I went to my door and took hold of the knob with two steady hands, just as a spy might do while attempting to break into a large safe. I turned the handle slowly to escape my father's notice as he read the newspaper in the living room, merely one flight of stairs below. After detecting the barely perceptible click, I carefully swung the door open just wide enough to crawl through — but not so far that a hinge might squeak, revealing my crime like a bank alarm. With cautious moves, I slipped across the hall to the bathroom, grabbed a metal hairdryer, and returned to my room before Dad even turned a page.

I continued my cunning as I wrapped the pillow around the hairdryer to muffle the noise. Mom's hair took only a few minutes to dry, so I knew this would be done pretty quickly. I plugged the cord into an outlet and went in my closet to search for a new activity.

Less than a minute later, the hairdryer's motor sounded different. As I turned to look, I noticed a pungent odor. My Styrofoam pillow appeared to have melted. So I did what any five-year-old might do when something seems too hot. I blew on it.

When my breath hit the smoldering material, my pillow glowed.

I ran from my room and bounded down the stairs, landing in the living room where my dad immediately began to lecture me that he had not yet said I could leave my room. He said all this and more still hidden behind his newspaper. Now I've always appreciated Dad's calm demeanor, even when scolding me, so I politely waited for him to finish. Finally, he asked why I had left my room without permission.

"Because I think my room is on fire," I said.

At the very moment that he lowered his newspaper to look at me, the pillow burst into flames, confirming my hunch. He ran up the stairs, grabbed the burning bundle, and threw it out my window. Amazingly, nothing else suffered damage — other than Dad's hands.

After Mom bandaged him up, and before he pronounced my new punishment, we talked about what had happened — a very one-way chat, as I recall. He asked why I had waited so long to say anything. Then he summed up an important lesson every child should learn: "Dave," he said, "you need to learn to speak up!"

Even without the extreme circumstance of a burning bedroom, inextinguishable truth remains. A child who is unable, unwilling, or unequipped to communicate with other people will struggle through life.

Please do not interpret this as an indictment of quiet personalities. I know plenty of soft-mannered children, including my own son and daughter, who nevertheless possess deep confidence to speak up. But no matter what the temperament or personality type, consider how a child will miss out on large portions of life if he or she struggles to engage people.

To help us understand what's at stake, author and pastor Greg Baker articulates four serious challenges parents can expect in this area. In his book *Fitly Spoken*, Baker says that poor expression skills can cause people to avoid you; make you seem unapproachable, leaving you with shallow relationships; haunt you in times of trouble, because no one will offer help; and result in an isolated life. Such an existence stands completely contrary to how God created you.[1] "It is not good for the man to be alone," said the Lord in Genesis 2:18.

Love one another. Serve one another. Greet, honor, be devoted to, live in harmony with, accept, instruct, be compassionate toward, speak to, submit to, and forgive one another. These New Testament expectations for how to live the way God wants us to live all require that people speak up and express themselves to one another.

So what holds people back? *They* do. More specifically, the culprit is what people think about their own abilities to interact and express thoughts, feelings, and opinions. Research from the University of New Mexico and West Virginia University that explores a concept called Willingness to Communicate (WTC) stresses the important role self-assessment plays: "If people do not perceive themselves as competent, it is presumed they would be both more likely to be apprehensive about communicating and to be less willing to engage in communicative behavior.... It is what a person thinks he/she can do, not what he/she actually could do, which impacts the individual's behavioral choices."[2]

So a child's willingness to communicate may well hinge on her belief in her own skill level? Yes. Another WTC research project from

West Virginia University — this one conducted in the everyday set-ting of the classroom — further proves this insight. "The results of this study," the report says, "while providing support for the validity of the WTC scale, also suggest that class participation may be in large part a function of an individual student's orientation toward commu-nication rather than a situation-specific response."[3]

Since children are more likely to speak up when parents have taught them to feel confident in their ability to express themselves, parents would be wise to focus on making this happen. And the first step toward this goal is as easy to see as a full moon on a clear night: convince kids that their opinions matter and that other people want to hear from them. Along the way, affirm them often as they express themselves. As a result, they'll dis-cover that speaking up becomes easier and that the world becomes surpris-ingly receptive to their thoughts — whether they know the answer to a math problem or believe their room has caught fire. To equip a child with such conviction requires guidance in two areas — assertiveness and appropriateness.

> Be strong and coura-geous. Do not be afraid; do not be discouraged, for the LORD your God will be with you wherever you go. (Joshua 1:9)

Assertiveness

According to healthy lifestyle guidelines published on the Mayo Clinic website, "Being assertive means that you express yourself effec-tively and stand up for your point of view, while also respecting the rights of others."[4] To help you teach your child how to develop this skill, we'll look at four general tips from the Mayo Clinic staff, then accompany those tips with coaching from focus-group parents and teens to help you put these ideas into practice.

1. Use "I" statements. Using "I" statements lets others know what you're thinking without sounding accusatory. For instance, say, "I disagree," rather than, "You're wrong."

Assertiveness begins with a child's ability to articulate what she thinks. Too often, kids learn to live with whatever Mom or Dad thinks about any and every situation. Bucking this trend, my wife, Becky, masterfully guides our children's development in this skill area by frequently asking, "What do you think about ____?" in conversations that require decisions. The confidence building becomes even more effective when she adds, "You have great ideas."

2. Practice saying no. If you have a hard time turning down requests, try saying, "No, I can't do that now." Don't beat around the bush—be direct.

While some situations call for a definitive no, other circumstances call for a wrong to be made right. A focus-group teenager shares what parental coaching of this sort looks like: "At restaurants when they don't get my order right, my dad makes *me* tell them," he says. "That helps me practice being able to stick up for myself."

3. Rehearse what you want to say. If it's challenging to say what you want or think, practice typical scenarios you encounter.

During the research conducted for this book, several parents mentioned the need to help children both rehearse and remember to use assertiveness skills. "We have to encourage one of our daughters to be what we call 'positively assertive,'" says Wynn, a mother of three. "Having a name to call it helped her know what to practice, and to remember to speak up and stand up for herself when the need arrived. A term for the idea helped to make it memorable."

4. Start small. At first, practice your new skills in low-risk situations.

At home in the company of family serves as the perfect low-risk place to start. A focus-group teen fondly shares how, in this setting, her parents coaxed her toward expression: "My parents always say

'Going once, going twice, gone!' to encourage me to say what I think. And it works."

Another useful technique was suggested by Ellen, whose family employs daily conversations to teach children to speak up and be heard. "Every night at dinner, we go around the table and ask everyone to share about their day," she says. "We include a rule that each person must say at least one thing, because we truly want to know about one another. This shows our kids that they are interesting when they talk, because we show interest in them when they do."

With her words "we truly want to know," Ellen describes an important component of encouraging kids' expression skills. Show a child authentic interest in her thoughts, her opinions, and her feelings, and she'll speak up more frequently. Try to fake authenticity or ignore its importance, though, and a child will begin to suspect that her expression has no value.

Encourage children enough, and speaking up will become a natural feature of your family life — and an attractive one. Peggy says, "Our kids' friends think our dinners and our home are fun because we encourage everyone to talk a lot. They say their own homes are too quiet."

While quietness has its own value, assertiveness will help children embrace more of what life has to offer. A focus-group teenager succinctly summarized why fellow students should want to demonstrate this attribute: "You could have some great ideas," she says, "but if you never speak up then those great ideas will be lost."

The apostle Paul had great ideas that, fortunately, he expressed. In the first verse of Acts 26, we find Paul under arrest and appearing before King Agrippa. The king says to Paul, "You have permission to speak for yourself," and the apostle delivers a powerful testimony that still inspires people more than two thousand years later.

Give your children permission to be assertive and speak for themselves.

Appropriateness

Laura recalls an evening when her six-year-old son spoke up. While she tried to hold a conversation with a houseguest, Nick frequently interrupted in an attempt to capture his mom's full attention. He had nothing urgent to share, only a desire to win his mom's undivided notice.

After their guest left, Laura lifted Nick onto a kitchen counter so they could talk eye-to-eye, a much different version of the undivided notice than this boy had craved earlier. "Nick, sometimes in life you just need to stay quiet and not say a word," she said, while maintaining a stern look.

Before she could continue, he asked, "Is this one of those times?"

To teach a child to speak up and be heard without any guidance as to what is appropriate is likely to backfire. Consider young Nick. Clearly he possesses confidence in his own ability to communicate. If he continues to inappropriately apply that skill, though, eventually others will feel annoyed by him — or possibly begin to ignore him. At some point, he'll sense that people either don't like him or don't want to hear what he has to say. Either way, a very real possibility exists that he will shut up and shut down.

> Those who guard their mouths and their tongues keep themselves from calamity. (Proverbs 21:23)

There are two perspectives to consider. First, call out your child when he inappropriately speaks up. Nick's mom served him well through their kitchen-counter chat immediately following his attention-seeking incident. Timely correction helps a child understand the transgression because he can still remember his specific actions.

At times, a child may truly be unaware that her remarks are inappropriate. "We're helping our daughter become more sensitive about expressing herself," says Stuart. "For example, a parent can get away with looking at a teenager's clothes and saying, 'You're not going out like that,' but my daughter believes she can say the same thing to us, her parents. She can't continue to just say whatever she wishes."

Second, encourage appropriate timing. Imagine the deep reinforcement that takes place when, after a conversation with another adult, you tell your son or daughter, "Way to go! You listened well, waited for your turn to talk, and spoke clearly when you had something to say."

Positive reinforcement will provide more valuable direction on appropriateness than correction ever could. Proverbs 22 instructs parents to "Train a child in the way he *should* go," [emphasis added] as opposed to focusing on mistakes (the way he *shouldn't* go).

The way your child should go extends well beyond the habits he or she demonstrates in your presence, a reality that may require parents to practice a bit of sleuthing. Evidence, though, may be more accessible than you think. "We point out and make a big deal of items on our kids' report cards other than just the grades," says Julie, "especially class participation marks."

Your child's school teacher, Sunday school teacher, and friends' parents all can serve as excellent sources of information about her communication tendencies and will give you plenty of direction toward areas to affirm or refine. Simply ask about your child's assertiveness and appropriateness. And, as with any lesson, remember that practice plays a big role. So think through how to provide regular, reliable times when a child knows she can speak up appropriately about whatever she wants while enjoying your full attention.

"Our sons talk the most when I tuck them into bed and say good night," says Mark. "That's been true when they were two and even when they were fifteen." This dad knows that he can display authentic interest and encourage his boys to speak their minds when he sets everything else aside and shares personal conversation. Especially when life's volume falls low enough for them to really listen to one another. This bedtime moment serves as a great end-of-day experience for his sons to sleep on— one that many kids can only dream about.

After all, willingness to communicate—to speak up and be heard—depends on your child's self-confidence. What he hears from you will either build up or tear down that confidence. As King Solomon said in Proverbs 18:21, "The tongue has the power of life and death, and those who love it will eat its fruit."

> For the mouth speaks what the heart is full of. (Matthew 12:34)

. . .

The words a person speaks can, however, work against him. "Do not let your mouth lead you into sin," Ecclesiastes 5:6 says. Sometimes this happens through speaking too much; other times, by what is said.

So in addition to quantity, word quality deserves parental vigil. Offensive language or putting others down presents an obvious target for correction. Another type of troublesome speech—stretching or misrepresenting the truth—presents itself as a more frequent, yet often subtle, problem that parents must address.

Only Speak the Truth

Honesty is the best policy—a kernel of universal wisdom that's frequently quoted but often ignored.

In theory, everyone agrees about the value of telling the truth. In practice, though, situations dictate whether or not many people speak honestly. Often, they lie. Left unchecked, all children will adopt this bad habit. I certainly did.

As a very average ten-year-old, I enjoyed discovering how things work. Especially anything that made loud noises, spiked my mom's blood pressure, or—as you're already aware—caught on fire.

For some reason, I felt drawn to answer a scientific question: If humidity really means water suspended in air, will matches burn in a room containing 100 percent humidity? A bathroom with the door closed and the shower running seemed like a perfect laboratory. Five matches later (scientifically valid results require multiple repetitions), I had my answer. Yes, they light and burn just fine.

About thirty minutes later, my dad called me and my older brother, Steve, to the family room. Apparently, all was not just fine. We sat on the couch while Dad sternly told us that he could smell something had burned in our house—and that the odor indicated matches. "Who did it?" he asked.

Silence.

"Somebody lit matches in the house, and you both know that's wrong," he said.

Not a word.

"The longer this goes on, the more trouble someone is in."

Still nothing.

"If no one admits to it soon, then you'll both receive punishment."

I couldn't take the pressure any longer, so I broke the silence and put an end to the charade when I said, "Steve did it."

A quick moment later, I learned two important facts. First, my mom had gone by the bathroom during my experiment. She knew the guilty party's identity all along. To her credit, her blood-pressure level seemed to have remained normal. Second, lies can burn a person more than any consequences that accompany the truth. Due to my blatant dishonesty, I believe I should still be serving time in my room.

Of all the lessons in this book, teaching kids to speak the truth seems the most obvious. Everyone knows it's wrong to lie, after all. So, then, why all the lies?

Dishonest talk began early in time, when Adam and Eve believed the serpent's lie and ate the fruit and then tried to bend the truth with God to escape trouble (Genesis 3).

Rather than simply blame the first man and woman for all this, though, let's hear from our focus-group parents about why today's kids avoid speaking the truth. Four main reasons emerged from the experiences of these veteran moms and dads. While all agreed that no one needs to worry about tall tales told by young children filled with imagination, honesty levels should increase as kids grow older—especially when they are directly asked for the truth. The first step in developing an effective approach to help children always speak the truth is to understand why they yield to the temptation to lie.

People Pleasing

Some children possess a great need to feel liked by other people. Unfortunately, this can cause them to avoid sharing anything less than positive news or calculated attempts to tell others what they want to hear. Parents can help such a child understand that the truth must come out by insisting on more information until the truth emerges. "Our son is a people pleaser, so he keeps things from us because he doesn't want to disappoint us," said Karyn. "We must keep prodding him to be more forthright. Many times we discover the truth only after asking several questions."

The child who places unusually high priority on feeling liked might also succumb to the temptation to tell "white" lies—fabrications justified by concern for other people's inability to handle the truth. Noble intent? Maybe. Good idea? No. A focus-group teenager articulates why: "Here's what I've learned; if you tell a white lie, you may get tangled in lies and trip over yourself. So the best thing is to always tell the truth."

Constantly remind a people-pleasing kid that you, and everyone else, will feel disappointed when he doesn't speak the truth. While that approach may sound harsh to some, it is an important step toward becoming a truth-teller.

Conflict Avoidance

The motivation to avoid speaking truth might come from an even more admirable character trait. Some children have tender hearts that genuinely prefer calm and harmony. "Our daughter doesn't tell the truth because she doesn't like arguments," says Karen.

Children like Karen's daughter typically don't tell blatant lies. According to focus-group parents, the more common approach is to fillet the truth—to use a few valuable pieces of what's accurate and discard the rest of the story. Jay knows exactly what this looks like and why it happens. "Our son became the master of half-truths because when he was young, I overreacted when he would tell me stuff," he says. "So he learned to mask the truth just enough to avoid a blow up, as an act of self-defense."

> Therefore confess your sins to each other and pray for each other so that you may be healed.
> (James 5:16)

The parental approach for such situations: stay in control of your reactions and emotions when your child speaks the truth, especially when he admits transgressions. Your response to a child will either encourage or discourage him to speak honestly as future issues arise.

Bad Influences

Your children learn about speaking the truth from you and from others. While you wield the greatest influence, yours is not an exclusive sway. As you think about your child's ability to speak honestly, consider who in her life might have conveyed a different lesson. "My two step-children had a mom who lied a lot, so they in turn lie a lot and believe it's normal," says Lynn.

In such cases, consistently extol truth's value and dishonesty's wrongness. Honest, direct, but respectful (of the errant person) conversation will help a child change much more than will an approach that involves attacking someone else's character.

Parental Modeling

"Honesty in my kids starts with me," says Jack.

Psychologists Dr. Henry Cloud and Dr. John Townsend would agree. "Teach your kids about truthfulness, require honesty from them, and properly correct any untruthfulness

> Do not be misled: "Bad company corrupts good character."
>
> (1 Corinthians 15:33)

they display. That's the first thing to worry about doing," they say. "Secondly, it's important to be a parent who is honest, does not give excuses, follows through on what you say you're going to do and is trustworthy."[5]

Jack knows that parental modeling is a full-time job. "Sometimes my wife and I will be in the middle of a sensitive conversation and a child will walk into our company and ask what we're talking about," he says. "So rather than lie about the topic, we say, 'It's private.'"

"It requires real work to not lie while also not sharing every piece of info with our children."

According to Jason, those who stand on a firm commitment to truth might occupy lonely property. "Many parents help their kids lie their way out of situations," he says. "I've known people who create fake family plans to help a child get out of an invitation she accepted and then changes her mind about. They teach their kids that it's okay to lie."

Moms and dads should, but often don't, maintain constant awareness that kids observe and mimic their parents' actions—regardless of any justification that surrounds those actions. So turn this reality into a positive opportunity. Let your children see your unwavering commitment to speak the truth and they will be much more likely to do the same.

Janice wishes she had adopted such a practice earlier. "I grew up as an exaggerator, and I didn't get over it until my thirties, when I noticed my daughter starting to do the same thing," she says. "Now I must constantly press her with questions like 'That sounds like you're using your imagination real well. So what *really* happened?'"

Develop a Habit

"The truth-telling issue is so hard to deal with," says Karen. "I wish I would have addressed it directly with my daughter when she was very young."

The most common coaching tip for Karen from focus-group parents: Help kids make truth-telling a habit. Paula articulated the consensus, most-likely-to-succeed approach. "We tell our kids, 'You won't get in trouble with us for a wrong act when you tell the truth, but you will *always* get in trouble if you lie,'" she says.

Those are easy words for parents to say and an attractive program for kids. Effectiveness, though, hinges on hard work for Mom and Dad—specifically, resisting the urge to dole out punishment when a child offers the truth about whatever he did. And to discipline dishonesty reliably whenever it happens. Consequences still occur for any transgression, meaning that even when a confession takes place, a child must apologize to a friend for hitting her, pay for a broken mirror, clean up a mess, or make any other restitution toward righting whatever is wrong. But the consequences shouldn't extend further, such as threatening to ground a kid until the age of fifty. (See the match/science experiment story).

Unless, of course, a child chooses dishonesty. "Our son lied about who he went to a movie with," says Julie. "The more times he denied what happened, the more privileges he lost. He learned that lying compounds trouble."

A focus-group teen offers clarity for the role honesty plays in a relationship: "If you lie, you are only lying to yourself and hurting others who trust and believe in you."

Early in a child's life, develop your own willingness to trade stiff punishments for the honesty habit. As that child grows, you'll trust her more when you believe she always tells you what *really* happens. Paula recently saw this trade pay off. "Our daughter did something wrong at school," she said, "and blurted out when she got in the car, 'I have to tell you something.'"

Trust is built and maintained through those six little words that every parent should love to hear: "I have to tell you something."

Worth It All

One afternoon a decade ago, my son, Scott, and I walked out of a hardware store toward our car. Something seemed wrong about our purchase, so I looked at the receipt and realized that the cashier had handed me too much change. Just as I had seen my dad do many years before, I went back into the store to return the extra cash. "Wasn't it his mistake?" Scott asked.

"Doesn't matter," I said. "It wouldn't be honest for me to keep the money. It's always best to do the right thing."

I can still remember the store clerk's shocked expression as I tried to hand him ten dollars. After insisting several times that he take the money, he acquiesced. Scott occasionally referred back to that episode, so it obviously made an impression on him. Years later, he confirmed that lesson's value.

During a high school parent-teacher conference, one of Scott's teachers said he had looked forward to telling me about a situation that happened in class two weeks earlier. He had my full attention.

Scott scored a perfect ten out of ten points on an assignment. After class, he returned the paper to the teacher and said that on the due date, he had not completed all the problems. The entire class discussed the assignment that day, and he made notes on the exercises he had failed to finish the night before. When the teacher collected the papers, it appeared that his had been complete at the start of class.

The teacher said Scott insisted that he only receive credit for the portion he completed on his own. Finally, the teacher relinquished and dropped his grade to five out of ten. "In all my years of teaching, he's the first student to demand a lower grade," he said. "I'm amazed."

I'd like to take credit for what happened. But to be perfectly honest, it started with my dad. He knew, you see, that honesty really *is* the best policy.

> The LORD detests lying lips, but he delights in people who are trustworthy.
>
> *Proverbs 12:22*

QUESTIONS FOR REFLECTION OR DISCUSSION

1. On a scale of 1 (silent) to 10 (obnoxious), rate your child's willingness to communicate with you ____, friends ____, other adults ____. You likely have three different ratings. In which area does she need help?
2. How committed is your child to honesty? How well have you emphasized speaking truthfully?
3. If asked, how would your child rate your commitment to honesty? What must you change to become a better model?

FAITH, HOPE, AND LOVE

The higher your structure is to be, the
deeper must be its foundation.
SAINT AUGUSTINE

In his early years, my son, Scott, loved Legos. I shared that love. Together, we built structures big and small. Mostly tall, though. Nearly every time we opened the tub filled with plastic press-together parts, we challenged ourselves to construct a tower taller than our previous best effort. The day we matched Scott's forty-two-inch height felt like quite an accomplishment. Upon the Christmas arrival of a larger version of Legos called Duplos, we embarked on a new, more aggressive goal—a tower as tall as Dad.

During construction, I held the structure at its midpoint to provide stability as Scott snapped one piece on top of another. Soon he needed a chair to continue building. Eventually, he believed our tower peaked at just the right height. He stepped off the chair and steadied the project so I could stand up for an official measurement. Scott had guessed right, a full three Duplos spanned above my head, topping out at over six feet.

We shouted for joy. We high-fived. We danced. Then, only a brief moment into our spontaneous celebration, the tower fell. No problem, we knew we could rebuild. From that moment on, though, construction projects always began with work on a stronger foundation.

Apparently, securing the base makes good design sense no matter what you're building. For example, the world's tallest structure, the Burj (tower) Khalifa in Dubai, stands 2,716 feet above the ground. To steady this amazing structure, the building rests upon 110,000 tons of concrete and steel that is 164 feet deep.[1]

From a Duplos tower to a Dubai skyscraper, a solid foundation matters.

All the previous lessons in this book help children develop life skills that will, with limits and balances, guide them well. Three lessons, though, rise above all others in importance. They require no counterparts, a big difference from the six lesson-pairs we have already covered. Together they form a deep, concrete-and-steel-like foundation to build upon.

The three: faith, hope, and love.

Ignore them, and your child will wobble when your steady hand is no longer in place to guide him. When these three qualities are buried deep into a child's life, though, they provide an anchor through turbulent times and a sturdy platform upon which a life can grow to heights worth celebrating—just as God designed.

Kid Lesson 1: Develop Your Own Faith

Several years ago, our family and a neighbor family formed a weekly small group. The other dad and I, sharing a burden to personally teach our children about faith, periodically met for breakfast to develop short Bible lessons.

One Sunday night, several months into our group meetings, he and I learned a valuable lesson. Not from one another, but from his daughter. The materials for that night, which we believed were both clever and compelling, focused on prayer. We creatively shared a Bible story, then spent the next several minutes describing prayer—what it means to us, how we do it, the joy of communicating directly with God, and more. All great stuff—to us, that is.

Quiet, nine-year-old Abby could endure our talking no longer. She took a deep breath and said, "Can we stop talking about praying and just pray?"

So we prayed.

That moment served as a turning point for those small group meetings. Prompted by Abby's boldness, our agenda became less about talk and more about action. Faith stopped existing as mere lessons and became real, through actions. We learned about prayer from praying. Learning about the importance of growing our hearts to serve others involved no lesson but consisted of actual serving projects—which grew our hearts. Jesus once said, "Let the little children come to me, and do not hinder them, for the kingdom of God belongs to such as these" (Matthew 19:14). Unfortunately, the natural instinct for many parents, myself included, looks more like "Tell your children about Jesus until they get it."

> Dear children, let us not love with words or speech but with actions and in truth.
> (1 John 3:18)

We discovered that our children learn more when we teach less and, instead, encourage them toward experience—to actually "come to" Jesus. Along the way, our kids' faith in God became their own. Not the faith of their fathers, which can feel more like rote memorization and reward, but faith deeply rooted in their own beliefs about God and a relationship with Jesus that they can personally embrace.

Numerous studies show that high numbers of young people walk away from their faith as they leave home following their teen years. What faith do they flee—their own? Not likely. The probable suspect is a faith that remains simply lessons, lectures, or long-winded parental talks. Full disclosure: I ran far away from anything to do with God after leaving home. At twenty-nine, I stopped running and found out Jesus was right there with me all along. But he never forced himself on me.

Likewise, parents who resort to force can't make a child believe. In his book *Here and Now*, Henri Nouwen says, "Life is a short opportunity each of us is given to say 'yes' to God."[2] While you and I long for our children to understand and grab hold of our beliefs, which seems like the shortest distance to yes, the only faith that they actually benefit from is that which they alone possess.

I fully understood the importance of a child owning a personal faith as I listened to my fourteen-year-old daughter's testimony before her baptism. She granted me permission to share her words exactly as she spoke them to our church congregation:

> Many years ago, I started learning about Jesus and that made me want to have Jesus become my best friend. Then one night I made a decision to have a relationship with him. In the years since I first made my decision to follow Jesus, I have learned lots about him and have become closer with him.
>
> That relationship became very important to me when I moved here [to Michigan] from Illinois a few years ago. I was the "new girl" at school, didn't have any friends and was sometimes lonely, but no matter how hard it got, I had Jesus with me.
>
> When I look back on the decision I made many years ago to follow Jesus, I never knew it would be the most important relationship these past couple of years. But now I know, when I face challenges in life, I have Jesus there with me.
>
> Today, I'm excited to get baptized and tell everyone that I have a relationship with Jesus.

Before she started to speak, I thought she might talk about the night I helped her pray to ask Jesus into her heart. I'm thrilled, though, that her most meaningful faith journey took place between just her and God. Here's why: when navigating life's difficult curves and sharp corners on her own, a child will either turn toward or away from God based on what *she* believes. It's up to her how *she* steers.

And that has very little to do with how Mom or Dad might react in similar circumstances.

In my tenure as a children's ministry director, parents often asked, "How can I know if my son has a personal faith?" Embedded deep in this question was their desire to feel complete confidence about their boy's standing with the Lord, for wishful thinking to become confident perspective. Martin Luther once said, "Faith is a living and unshakable confidence, a belief in the grace of God so assured that a man would die a thousand deaths for its sake."[3] I took a much simpler approach and asked, "Can your child talk about what he believes, in his own words, and does he act differently because of those beliefs?"

As the world becomes a tougher place for children—more alluring, more hostile, more filled with challenges, opportunities to feel disappointment, and peer pressure—how important is it for a child to possess a personal faith? Hebrews 11:1 in *The Message* translation answers that question when it tells us that faith is "the firm foundation under everything that makes life worth living."

Kid Lesson 2: Face Life Filled With Hope

Oscar Hammerstein II once said, "It is a modern day tragedy that despair has so many spokesmen, and hope so few."[4] His observation could help explain why, according to the Centers for Disease Control, in any two-week period a staggering 4.3 percent of youth ages twelve to seventeen experience depression.[5] The CDC also reports that 14.5 percent of high school students have seriously considered suicide in the previous twelve months, and that 6.9 percent of students reported at least one such attempt in that same time frame.[6]

While this nationwide problem might seem too extreme for most parents to relate to, many parents of the children represented in those statistics likely felt the same way. Two thousand students attend the high school just a block from our house. Considering the CDC statistics, almost 300 seriously considered taking their lives over the past year, and nearly 140 actually tried. In the past fourteen days, depression's grip will have squeezed 86 more kids. Some of them will attend our church youth group, visit the coffee shop I frequent, maybe even say hello to me. I likely know the parents of a few.

Consider your own community for a moment. Do the math.

Despair continues to collect wins because too many children suffer from hope anemia — a deficit that often begins before their high school years. Home by home, hope needs more spokesmen — to children of all ages.

How high is your child's hope level? If I flippantly ignore the potential for depression and despair to sink their eager teeth into my children, then who will keep watch and do battle?

To clarify, hope is belief and trust in something better. In possibility. In positive change. When a child faces life filled with hope, he knows that current circumstances are temporary, that setbacks aren't reason to give up, and that real potential always exists for life to improve — maybe all the way to extraordinary. The resulting message of such knowledge is to keep going, keep going.

Parents help a child develop such an approach to life by acknowledging disappointment, but then pointing him toward a hope-filled path. Over and over and over again. Sports teams make late-in-the-game comeback victories because the hope of a win stays with them. Sometimes, even when they fall short, they can still emerge as winners.

My son, Scott, worked hard this past winter and spring to further develop his quarterback skills. He entered the dreaded two-a-day practice season for his high school team with great anticipation for the season ahead. Just nine days before the season began, after making it through the worst-of-the-worst grueling practices, his elbow snapped as he threw a routine pass.

An initial X-ray failed to detect the break. Filled with hope that the injury would soon pass, Scott continued to practice hard. Three weeks later, an orthopedic surgeon found the fracture and said the elbow needed three more weeks to heal. So Scott continued to practice with the team—his comeback now in sight. Unfortunately, the team lost their initial playoff game so the season ended before Scott could regain strength to throw. Despite the circumstances, his hope in something better, in the possibility for the season to turn around, kept him going.

Cynics would say he wasted his time. Critics would chide my wife and me for the many hours we spent encouraging him. They fail to see, though, what a parent can see: a young man whose hope refused to yield to despair. What a victory!

Hope does not involve denial, so resist any urge to minimize big setbacks your child will face. Disappointment is a reality that all kids must encounter and work through. But the important thing is to keep moving through difficult times. "Hope is the indispensible fuel for all human action," says pastor and author John Ortberg. "When hope dies, motivation dies. There is no longer any reason to try anything. But once hope enters [a child's heart], anything is possible."[7]

But hope in what? Grand accomplishment? All-American status? Fame and fortune? No, something better. God's plan and purpose for our lives. Jeremiah 29:11 communicates this truth: "'For I know the plans I have for you,' declares the LORD, 'plans to prosper you and not to harm you, plans to give you hope and a future.'"

> Many are the plans in a person's heart, but it is the LORD's purpose that prevails. (Proverbs 19:21)

A child filled with belief that life happens according to the plans God architected just for him will plow through circumstances thick and thin. A parent who consistently reminds her child of this truth teaches a powerful lesson.

While the world in which we live contains a multitude of characters eager to put a child down, a single person can give a child enough hope to keep pressing forward. As Darren prepared to graduate from high school, he hand-delivered a commencement invitation to his elementary school mentor. "Miss Nancy, thank you," he said. "You were the only one who didn't believe I was too stupid to learn."

Just one adult, passionate to help a child believe that something better can happen, can fill a young heart with hope. As a result, that child's future will grow from a stronger foundation and life will overflow with possibilities.

Kid Lesson 3: Live to Love God and Others

In Betsy Taylor's book *What Kids Really Want That Money Can't Buy*, an eloquent eleven-year-old named Meleek says, "The one thing that I want is love. Love from my family, and love from the people who know me best."[8]

This young man articulates a key truth. To thrive, a child must *receive* love. But that's just the start.

In Matthew 22:37–39, Jesus says that to *share* love is the highest purpose and mission for life: " 'Love the Lord your God with all your heart and with all your soul and with all your mind.' This is the first and greatest commandment. And the second is like it: 'Love your neighbor as yourself.' "

Curious, isn't it? Jesus offers extreme clarity about what really matters. At the same time, society ferociously attempts to lure children into a life spent chasing material and temporal success. Love self? Definitely. What about God and others? Maybe for a little while on Sundays. But only maybe. Children need parents willing to teach them the lesson they need to learn most—that nothing is more important than orienting your entire life around loving God and people.

Before placing a check mark in the "I do this" box in your mind, let's look at this lesson closer. We covered the "love God" portion of

Jesus' command earlier, in the "Develop Your Own Faith" section. So now let's turn our attention to the love-people half.

Many children hear from their parents about the importance of a loving attitude toward others, which typically involves acting nice, eliminating the word "hate," using polite words, and avoiding trouble. Some go on to learn about the value of expressing love. But in 1 John 3:18, the Bible says: "Dear children, let us not love with words or speech, but with actions and in truth."

Teach your children this command about love because actions speak louder than words.

In *Mere Christianity*, C.S. Lewis takes this concept a step further, writing, "The rule for all of us is perfectly simple. Do not waste time bothering whether you 'love' your neighbor; act as if you did. As soon as we do this we find one of the great secrets. When you are behaving as if you loved someone, you will presently come to love him."[9]

This lesson, the most important one between the covers of this book, is easy to teach. Go across the street and welcome the new family, and make sure you take your child with you. Rake someone else's leaves, shovel their snow, run an errand for them—all these activities serve as hands-on instruction opportunities.

For more advanced training, consider the deliberate lesson that Greg, Lisa, and their two children—along with another family of four—recently experienced. This eight-person team arranged to serve dinner on Christmas Eve at a local shelter for women and children. Instead of having residents walk through a food line with trays, the two families asked everyone to sit at tables and enjoy a meal personally served to them.

In preparation for the evening, the two families had prepared gift bags for the children. Nothing fancy, the bags included candy, stickers, and a few other small play items. And, of course, candy canes. For many, the bag would be their only gift.

While Greg, Lisa, and the team cleaned the kitchen, one of the moms told them that the gift bags were special because her kids could personally say thank you. Everyone exchanged smiles and hugs, and the two families left to attend a late Christmas Eve service. All eight felt their hearts ready to burst with joy as they heard the words "I bring you good news of great joy" (Luke 2:10) because earlier that evening, they had experienced amazing joy.

In 1 Corinthians 13, the apostle Paul teaches that love serves as a critical element of life. In fact, the most important ingredient. Without it, little else matters. Parents show great wisdom when they start the lessons their kids need to learn with Paul's conclusion: "Now these three remain; faith, hope, and love. And the greatest of these is love."

> As for everyone who comes to me and hears my words and
> puts them into practice, I will show you what they are like.
> They are like a man building a house, who dug down deep
> and laid the foundation on rock. When a flood came, the
> torrent struck that house but could not shake it, because it was
> well built.
>
> *Luke 6:47–48*

QUESTIONS FOR REFLECTION OR DISCUSSION

1. While in a relaxed conversation, ask your child to articulate his faith. Suggestions for nonthreatening questions: "How would you describe a relationship with Jesus?" or "If you could tell a friend about God, what would you say?"

2. What aspirations does your child have? Does your child believe, or roll his eyes at, Jeremiah 29:11? Describe for your child what this verse means to you, especially when faced with difficulties.

3. List the last few acts of love your family did for someone else. Was this list easy to write? If not, decide on at least three specific ways that your family will show love for others, and then follow through on that plan.

A FINAL WORD

By Scott Staal

Adults often tell us kids what to do. Many school teachers do that all day long. Truthfully, most of us pay attention to only part of what they say—and ignore their large volumes of irrelevant or impractical words. The best teachers, though, *show* more than they *tell*.

The same goes for parents. Moms and dads can talk a good game and (endlessly) instruct their kids, but when they actually live out a lesson, kids will start to listen—and to follow that lesson.

True to form, the message "actions speak louder than words" might come across as dull to read about on its own. So instead of writing a final word, I'll share a final lesson—one that hopefully shows more than it tells. Recently, my dad taught me about humility. The lesson was based on how the Bible defines humility, "Do not think of yourself more highly than you ought" (Romans 12:3). It happened when he told me, "Scott, no matter how high you climb in life, never be too good to take out the trash."

That was the *tell*. Here comes the *show*.

Was his word choice fancy, or did he read this saying off of a bumper sticker? Neither. Dad's words weren't real clever. Fairly forgettable, honestly. But there were two important reasons why this lesson will always stick with me.

First, my dad works as the president of an organization—I consider that as "climbing high in life." Second, and most important, he told me those words on a Saturday afternoon while he helped me take out the trash in the office building where he works, which is *my* part-time job on weekends.

As you reflect back on all the lessons that you learned in this book, some most likely stood out more than others. Want to know how to successfully approach your kids with these lessons? First, model what you want them to do. Only then will you be able to guide with your words. That approach works for me, and it will work for your son or daughter too.

I'm not sure if I will ever become an organization's president. But no matter what I do, I will always remember that I'm never too important to take out the trash. Thanks, Dad.

If you want to see the amazing difference your actions will make as you teach your son or daughter, then be deliberate. Resist the urge to simply tell them something and, instead, look for ways to show it to them. In this way, you'll find life filled with opportunities to teach — and model — the lessons your kids need to learn.

ACKNOWLEDGMENTS

Becky—Thanks for partnering with me on this book, in parenting, and for life. The focus groups succeeded because of you, the kids thrive because of you, and our love continues to grow because of you.

Scott—Thanks for sharing a piece of your heart, and your writing talent, in the "Final Word." I feel proud and amazed at the young man you've become. I love you.

Erin—Thanks for the incredible work you did that made the student focus groups a massive win for the book. Your talent, creativity, and humor bring me intense joy. I will always love you.

Judy—Thanks for sharing your world-class talent, patience, and grace. I cherish our relationship.

Parent Focus-Group Participants—Thanks for your willingness to share what worked and what didn't work. Your experiences will make a difference for all who read this book.

Student Focus-Group Participants—Thanks for your honesty and willingness to take a chance and give your comments. I hope it feels good to know you helped teach parents.

Ryan and the Zondervan team—Thanks for believing in this book idea and for partnering in ways that make writing a thrill. Not the editing, just the writing.

KIDS HOPE USA staff—Thanks for making the journey to reach kids an amazing adventure. I appreciate your patience, enthusiastic support, and sense of humor.

KIDS HOPE USA volunteers—Thanks for loving kids so deeply

that anyone who watches feels inspired to change a life. And that's no small change.

Steve—Thanks for the prayers, encouragement, and friendship.

Becky—Two acknowledgements to make one point clear: I love you.

ENDNOTES

Chapter 1: Pairs, Parents, and Kids

1. Carol S. Dweck, *Mindset* (New York: Ballantine, 2008), 176.
2. Jay Allison and Dan Gediman, eds., *This I Believe* (New York: Henry Holt, 2006), xx.
3. Gilbert Cruz, "Parent Academies," *Time* (November 16, 2009), 52.

Chapter 2: Believe That You Matter / Live Like Others Matter More

1. Ralph Waldo Emerson, *The Complete Prose Works of Ralph Waldo Emerson* (Whitefish, Mont.: Kessinger, 2007), 472.
2. Mike Singletary, *Daddy's Home at Last* (Grand Rapids, Mich.: Zondervan, 1998), 185.
3. Nancy Gibbs, "The Magic of the Family Meal," *Time* (June 4, 2006), www.time.com/time/magazine/article/0,9171,1200760,00.html.
4. National Center on Addiction and Substance Abuse at Columbia University, "The Importance of Family Dinners," (September 23, 2009), www.casacolumbia.org/templates/publications_reports.aspx.
5. John from Bridgewater, Mass., "The Fear That I Don't Matter," *This I Believe* (March 16, 2006), www.thisibelieve.org/essay/11793/.

6. Samuel L. Clemens, *Mark Twain's Notebook*, ed. Albert Bigelow Paine (New York: Harper and Brothers, 1935), 343.

7. James Robinson, *A Dad's Blessing* (Nashville, Tenn.: J. Countryman, 2005), 21.

8. Larry King, *My Dad and Me* (New York: Crown, 2006), 84.

Chapter 3: Appreciate Those Who Serve You / Make Serving Others a Priority

1. Larry King, *My Dad and Me* (New York: Crown, 2006), 88.

2. Catalyst 2009 Compassion Moment (Atlanta, GA: Catalyst Conference, 2009), www.catalystspace.com/catablog/full/2009_catalyst_compassion_moment/.

3. "Undercover Lunch Lady: Do Kids Use Manners?" (Minneapolis, MN: CBS WCCO-TV, May 24, 2010), www.wcco.com/parenting/kids.use.manners.2.1712717.html.

4. Bill Robinson, *Incarnate Leadership* (Grand Rapids, Mich.: Zondervan, 2009), 104–5.

5. Eloise Parker, "Teaching Kids about the Gift of Saying 'Thank You' May Have Health Benefits" (NYDailyNews.com, November 17, 2007), www.nydailynews.com/lifestyle/health/2007/11/17/2007-11-17_teaching_kids_about_the_gift_of_saying_t-1.html.

6. Deirdre Sullivan, "Always Go to the Funeral," *This I Believe: The Personal Philosophies of Remarkable Men and Women*, eds. Jay Allison and Dan Gediman (New York: Holt, 2007), 237.

7. John Ortberg, *The Me I Want to Be* (Grand Rapids, Mich.: Zondervan, 2010), 187.

Chapter 4: Forget Unimportant Stuff / Remember Life Has Consequences

1. John Cloud, "Staying Sane May Be Easier Than You Think," *Time* (June 22, 2009), 72.

2. Jeanne Phillips, "Dear Abby" (*uexpress.com,* August 23, 2009), www.uexpress.com/dearabby/?uc_full_date=20090823.

3. Lenore Skenazy, *Free Range Kids* (San Francisco: Jossey-Bass, 2009), 182.

4. Insurance industry general information (Tigard, Ore.: Health Source NW, 2010), healthsourcenw.com/faq.html.

5. "USU Technology is Finalist in 2009 'Concept To Company' Contest," press release, Utah State University, Nov. 19, 2009.

6. Cloud, *Time* (June 22, 2009), 72.

7. Facebook Data Team, "Maintained Relationships on Facebook," *Facebook.com* March 9, 2009, www.facebook.com/notes.php?id=8394258414.

8. Kathy Slobogin, "Survey: Many Students Say Cheating's OK," *CNN.* April 5, 2002, www.archives.cnn.com/2002/fyi/teachers.ednews/04/05/highschool.cheating/index.html.

9. Ibid.

10. Ellen Greenberger, "Self-Entitled College Students: Contributions of Personality, Parenting, and Motivational Factors," *Journal of Youth Adolescence* (April 4, 2008), 37.

11. Tim Clinton and Gary Sibcy, *Loving Your Child Too Much* (Franklin, Tenn.: Integrity, 2006), 101–3.

12. Ibid, 103.

13. Slobogin. *Survey.*

14. National Institute on Drug Abuse, "High School and Youth Trends," *NIDA Info Facts,* January 2010, www.drugabuse.gov/infofacts/infofactsindex.html/.

15. Claudia Wallis, "The Myth About Homework," *Time* (August 29, 2006), www.time.com/time/magazine/article/0,9171,1376208,00.html/.

16. "Daily Media Use Among Children and Teens Up Dramatically From Five Years Ago," news release, January 20, 2010, www.kff.org/entmedia/entmedia012010nr.cfm.

17. Marcus Buckingham, *The One Thing You Need to Know* (New York: Free Press, 2005), 79.

18. James Baldwin, *Baldwin: Collected Essays*, ed. Toni Morrison, (New York: Library of America, 1998), 173.

Chapter 5: Be a People Person / Be Your Own Person

1. Eds. Allison and Gediman, *This I Believe*, 125.

2. Rachel Zupek, "The Worst Way to Shake Hands," *Career-Builder.com*, August 1, 2007, www.cnn.com/2007/LIVING/worklife/11/05/cb.hand.shake/index.html.

3. "Newborns Can Detect Eye Movement," *BBC News World Edition*, June 25, 2002, news.bbc.co.uk/2/hi/health/2064659.stm.

4. Peter Newhouse, weekend message at Watermark Church, Grand Haven, Mich., 2010.

5. Alex Harris and Brett Harris, *Do Hard Things* (Colorado Springs: Multnomah, 2008), 153.

6. Brent A. Scott and Timothy A. Judge, "The Popularity Contest at Work: Who Wins, Why, and What Do They Receive?" *Journal of Applied Psychology* 94, no. 1 (2009): 20–33.

Chapter 6: Find Your Unique Fit / Find Out You Can Fail

1. Megan Clinton, *Totally God's 4 Life Devotional* (Eugene, Ore.: Harvest House, 2009), 75.

2. Maria Shriver, *Ten Things I Wish I'd Known—Before I Went Out into the Real World* (New York: Warner Books, 2000), 63.

3. Sinem Siyahhan, Sasha Barab, and Carrie James, "Youth and the Ethics of Identity Play in Virtual Spaces," www.inkido.indiana.edu/research/onlinemanu/papers/identityplay.pdf.

4. Mike Robbins, *Be Yourself, Everyone Else is Already Taken: Transform Your Life with the Power of Authenticity* (San Francisco: Jossey-Bass, 2009), 115.

5. Carol S. Dweck, "The Secret to Raising Smart Kids," *Scientific American Mind* (Nov. 28, 2007), 36.

6. Jim Taylor, "Fear of Failure: A Childhood Epidemic," 2005, www.keepkidshealthy.com/parenting_tips/fear_of_failure. html.

7. Carla Harris, *Expect to Win: Proven Strategies for Success from a Wall Street Vet* (New York: Hudson Street Press, 2009), 150.

8. Taylor, "Fear of Failure."

9. Nancy Gibbs, "The Case Against Over-Parenting," *Time* (November 30, 2009).

10. Ibid.

11. Dweck, *Mindset*, 175.

12. Senator Barack Obama speech, Campus Progress Annual Conference (July 12 2006), transcript accessed at www. asksam.com/ebooks/releases.asp?file=Obama-Speeches. ask&dn=Campus%20Progress%20Annual%20Conference.

13. Thomas McDade, public release, "Think Again about Keeping Little Ones So Squeaky Clean" (Evanston, Ill.: Northwestern University, December 8, 2009).

14. Randy Pausch, *The Last Lecture* (New York: Hyperion, 2008), 148.

Chapter 7: Always Speak Up / Only Speak the Truth

1. Greg S. Baker, *Fitly Spoken* (www.fitlyspoken.org, 2010), 33.

2. Robert A. Barraclough, Diane M. Christophel, James C. McCroskey, "Willingness to Communicate: A Cross-Cultural Investigation," *Communication Research Reports* 5, no. 2 (1988): 187–92.

3. Betty Chan and James C. McCroskey, "The WTC Scale As a Predictor of Classroom Participation," *Communication Research Reports* 4, no 2 (1987): 47–50.

4. Mayo Clinic Staff, "Being Assertive: Reduce Stress, Communicate Better," *Mayo Clinic*, June 17, 2009, www.mayoclinic.com/ health/assertive/SR00042.

5. Dr. Henry Cloud and Dr. John Townsend, "Raising Great Kids: The Santa Claus Debate," Christianity Today/MOMSense, 2009, www.christianitytoday.com/momsense/2009/novdec/raisinggreatkids.html.

Chapter 8: Faith, Hope, and Love

1. Specification from Emporis (Frankfurt, Germany), http://www.emporis.com/application/?nav=building&lng=3&id=burjdubai-dubai-unitedarabemirates.

2. Henri Nouwen, *Here and Now* (New York: Crossroad, 1994), 171.

3. MartI usein Luther, "Preface to his translation of St. Paul's Epistle to the Romans (1522)," *International Thesaurus of Quotations* (New York: HarperCollins, 1996), 214.

4. Allison and Gediman, *This I Believe*, 106.

5. Laura A. Pratt, Ph.D. and Debra J. Brody, M.P.H., "Depression in the United States Household Population, 2005–2006," *NCHS Data Brief No. 7* (Centers for Disease Control and Prevention, September 2008).

6. Centers for Disease Control, "Suicide: Facts at a Glance," (Centers for Disease Control, 2009), www.cdc.gov/violenceprevention.

7. John Ortberg, "Holding Out Hope," *Leadership Journal.net*, April 27, 2009, www.christianitytoday.com/le/2008/fall/holdingouthope.html.

8. Betsy Taylor, *What Kids Really Want That Money Can't Buy* (New York: Warner, 2003), 149.

9. C. S. Lewis, *Mere Christianity* (New York: Macmillan, 1960), 101.

Words Kids Need to Hear

To Help Them Be Who God Made Them to Be

David Staal

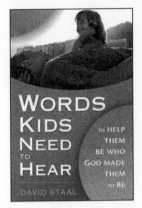

Words matter. Words can build up, or words can tear down. As parents and church leaders, do we use our words well? *Words Kids Need to Hear* offers compelling, yet simple ways to build up the hearts of children through meaningful and well-chosen words. What children hear from adults they trust makes a significant impact—now and for years to come.

Words Kids Need to Hear offers an easy-to-follow learning path. Each of the seven chapters focuses on a single statement kids need to hear from parents, children's workers, and other close adults. These seven statements are simple to share, yet guaranteed to make a profound impact on a child's life. They are: "I Believe in You," "You Can Count on Me," "I Treasure You," "I'm Sorry, Please Forgive Me," "Because," "No," "I Love You."

Words Kids Need to Hear helps parents and children's workers use words to build up the hearts of elementary-age children, resulting in closer parent-child relationships that pave a path toward a relationship with God.

Making Your Children's Ministry the Best Hour of Every Kid's Week

Sue Miller with David Staal

Promiseland is Willow Creek's highly successful children's ministry. Using examples from Promiseland and churches of all sizes around the country, this book provides step-by-step guidance and creative application exercises to help churches develop a thriving children's ministry—one that strives to be the best hour of every kid's week. Included are Scripture-based principles and practical resources for church staff members and volunteers who agree with the critical role children's ministry plays in a local church.

Making Your Children's Ministry the Best Hour of Every Kid's Week, based on twenty-eight years of experience at Willow Creek, explains four ministry foundations: Mission, Vision, Values, and Strategy.

Available in stores and online!

Leading Your Child to Jesus

How Parents Can Talk with Their Kids about Faith

David Staal

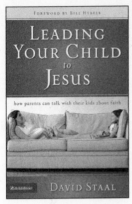

What will you say when your child asks how Jesus can fit inside his heart?

Here's help with responding in words your little one will understand. *Leading Your Child to Jesus* equips you with the simple, effective communication tools that will help you discuss salvation with your child. They've been proven through David Staal's years with Willow Creek Community Church's Promiseland children's ministry and through his personal experiences as a parent.

Learn how to share your own salvation story, explain the gospel in kid-friendly language, and lead your child in a prayer of salvation. Based on examples from the book of Acts, *Leading Your Child to Jesus* provides you with key biblical concepts on effective communication and includes exercises to help you put those concepts into action.